St. Mary's High School

INTRODUCING
ISSUES WITH
OPPOSING
VIEWPOINTS®

Globalization

Noël Merino, *Book Editor*

GREENHAVEN PRESS
A part of Gale, Cengage Learning

GALE
CENGAGE Learning™

Detroit • New York • San Francisco • New Haven, Conn • Waterville, Maine • London

Christine Nasso, *Publisher*
Elizabeth Des Chenes, *Managing Editor*

For more information, contact:
Greenhaven Press
27500 Drake Rd.
Farmington Hills, MI 48331-3535
Or you can visit our Internet site at gale.cengage.com

Articles in Greenhaven Press anthologies are often edited for length to meet page requirements. In addition, original titles of these works are changed to clearly present the main thesis and to explicitly indicate the author's opinion. Every effort is made to ensure that Greenhaven Press accurately reflects the original intent of the authors. Every effort has been made to trace the owners of copyrighted material.

Cover image by Romeo Gacad/AFP/Getty Images

LIBRARY OF CONGRESS CATALOGING-IN-PUBLICATION DATA
Globalization / Noël Merino, editor.
p. cm. -- (Introducing issues with opposing viewpoints)
Includes bibliographical references and index.
ISBN 978-0-7377-4476-7 (hardcover)
1. Globalization--Juvenile literature. I. Merino, Noël.
JZ1318.G56427 2009
303.48'2--dc22
2009023850

Printed in the United States of America
1 2 3 4 5 6 7 13 12 11 10 09

Contents

Chapter 3: What Are Some Concerns About Globalization?

Foreword

I ndulging in a wide spectrum of ideas, beliefs, and perspectives is a critical cornerstone of democracy. After all, it is often debates over differences of opinion, such as whether to legalize abortion, how to treat prisoners, or when to enact the death penalty, that shape our society and drive it forward. Such diversity of thought is frequently regarded as the hallmark of a healthy and civilized culture. As the Reverend Clifford Schutjer of the First Congregational Church in Mansfield, Ohio, declared in a 2001 sermon, "Surrounding oneself with only like-minded people, restricting what we listen to or read only to what we find agreeable is irresponsible. Refusing to entertain doubts once we make up our minds is a subtle but deadly form of arrogance." With this advice in mind, Introducing Issues with Opposing Viewpoints books aim to open readers' minds to the critically divergent views that comprise our world's most important debates.

Introducing Issues with Opposing Viewpoints simplifies for students the enormous and often overwhelming mass of material now available via print and electronic media. Collected in every volume is an array of opinions that captures the essence of a particular controversy or topic. Introducing Issues with Opposing Viewpoints books embody the spirit of nineteenth-century journalist Charles A. Dana's axiom: "Fight for your opinions, but do not believe that they contain the whole truth, or the only truth." Absorbing such contrasting opinions teaches students to analyze the strength of an argument and compare it to its opposition. From this process readers can inform and strengthen their own opinions, or be exposed to new information that will change their minds. Introducing Issues with Opposing Viewpoints is a mosaic of different voices. The authors are statesmen, pundits, academics, journalists, corporations, and ordinary people who have felt compelled to share their experiences and ideas in a public forum. Their words have been collected from newspapers, journals, books, speeches, interviews, and the Internet, the fastest growing body of opinionated material in the world.

Introducing Issues with Opposing Viewpoints shares many of the well-known features of its critically acclaimed parent series, Opposing Viewpoints. The articles are presented in a pro/con format, allowing readers to absorb divergent perspectives side by side. Active reading questions preface each viewpoint, requiring the student to approach the material thoughtfully and carefully. Useful charts, graphs, and cartoons supplement each article. A thorough introduction provides readers with crucial background on an issue. An annotated bibliography points the reader toward articles, books, and Web sites that contain additional information on the topic. An appendix of organizations to contact contains a wide variety of charities, nonprofit organizations, political groups, and private enterprises that each hold a position on the issue at hand. Finally, a comprehensive index allows readers to locate content quickly and efficiently.

Introducing Issues with Opposing Viewpoints is also significantly different from Opposing Viewpoints. As the series title implies, its presentation will help introduce students to the concept of opposing viewpoints and learn to use this material to aid in critical writing and debate. The series' four-color, accessible format makes the books attractive and inviting to readers of all levels. In addition, each viewpoint has been carefully edited to maximize a reader's understanding of the content. Short but thorough viewpoints capture the essence of an argument. A substantial, thought-provoking essay question placed at the end of each viewpoint asks the student to further investigate the issues raised in the viewpoint, compare and contrast two authors' arguments, or consider how one might go about forming an opinion on the topic at hand. Each viewpoint contains sidebars that include at-a-glance information and handy statistics. A Facts About section located in the back of the book further supplies students with relevant facts and figures.

Following in the tradition of the Opposing Viewpoints series, Greenhaven Press continues to provide readers with invaluable exposure to the controversial issues that shape our world. As John Stuart Mill once wrote: "The only way in which a human being can make some approach to knowing the whole of a subject is by hearing what can be said about it by persons of every variety of opinion and studying all modes in which it can be looked at by every character of mind. No wise man ever acquired his wisdom in any mode but this." It is to this principle that Introducing Issues with Opposing Viewpoints books are dedicated.

Introduction

"The pace of global economic change in recent decades has been breathtaking indeed, and the full implications of these developments for all aspects of our lives will not be known for many years. History may provide some guidance, however."

—Ben S. Bernanke, chairman of the
Federal Reserve, August 25, 2006

Globalization is a process whereby economic, political, social, and cultural differences are lessened by greater interaction across national boundaries. Greater international interaction in the past several decades has been due to a variety of factors that, on the whole, can be seen as eliminating the barriers of distance. The current wave of globalization, occurring from the second half of the twentieth century to today, is considered to be the most extensive in history, though notable globalization has occurred during other periods. The speed and scope of this most recent wave of globalization has led to much debate about the effects of such rapid change.

In its broadest sense the term "globalization" simply means the process of making anything more global, whether it be the worldwide availability of products such as Coca-Cola or the growth of international entities such as the World Trade Organization (WTO). As linguist Noam Chomsky notes, although "in its literal sense, 'globalization' means international integration," it is often used to describe a particular set of principles or guidelines for international economic policy that favors the removal of barriers to trade and foreign investment. In the view of critics of globalization, as defined in this specific way, such policy favors "investors, financial institutions and other sectors of power, with the interests of people incidental."[1] In the opinion of those who favor the policy as it is defined here, "globalization raises the productivity and living standards of people in countries that open themselves to the global marketplace."[2] Thus, in the current debates for and against globalization, it is this more narrow understanding of globalization that involves a commitment to certain economic policies.

The British East India Company was founded at the beginning of the seventeenth century and is an early example of globalization efforts.

Although the term "globalization" is a relatively new one, the process of integration across national boundaries is one that has occurred at several notable points in history. For instance, during the last two thousand years, explorers set out to find new lands and, in the process, discovered foreign people who had unique goods to trade. Trade itself is a major factor of globalization, as it leads to the exchange of goods, culture, language, and, often, the migration of people. One historical example is that of the British East India Company, founded at the beginning of the seventeenth century, after explorers had returned from India in the previous century. The company traded in goods from India, such as cotton and tea, and such trade resulted not only in the trade of goods but also in the exchange of cultural practices, the sharing of language, and human migration.

The company was more than just a trading company. It ruled India from 1757 to 1858, followed by the ruling of India by the British monarchy for almost another century prior to India's gaining its independence from Britain in 1947. The company that goes by the same name today claims that some of the positive influences the East India Company had on India included establishing the present education system, spreading the English language, and laying the groundwork for India's present banking and financial systems.[3] Some critics of globalization would say that the history of the East India Company reflects too well some of the current concerns about globalization:

Today, we can see the East India Company as the first "imperial corporation," the very design of which drove it to market domination, speculative excess, and the evasion of justice. Like the modern multinational, it was eager to avoid the mere interplay of supply and demand. It jealously guarded its chartered monopoly of imports from Asia. But it also wanted to control the sources of supply by breaking the power of local rulers in India and eliminating competition so that it could force down its purchase prices.[4]

Though the East India Company operated in a time very different from ours—without the speed of communication offered by phones and computers, and without the speed offered by modern transportation—the basic way in which globalization was driven in the seventeenth century is still relevant today. The demand for certain goods around the world creates a market for global trade and, thus, the opportunity for large international companies to do business in many different countries. One debate that arises out of the business practices of multinational companies concerns the appropriate balance between protecting national economies and allowing access to trade among countries of different wealth and development status. These issues, as well as others concerning the benefits and harms of globalization to nations around the world, are explored in *Introducing Issues with Opposing Viewpoints: Globalization.*

Notes

1. Noam Chomsky, "Chat with Chomsky," *Washington Post,* March 24, 2006. www.washingtonpost.com/wp-dyn/content/discussion/2006/03/14/DI2006031400824.html.
2. Cato Institute's Center for Trade Policy Studies, "The Benefits of Globalization," 2009. www.freetrade.org/issues/globalization.html.
3. British East India Company, "History (1600–Present)." www.thebritish eastindiacompany.com/history.html.
4. Nick Robins, "The World's First Multinational," *New Statesman,* December 13, 2004. www.newstatesman.com/200412130016.htm.

Chapter 1

Is Globalization Good for Americans?

Workers in New York City protest the globalization of industry. Whether or not globalization is good for Americans is a highly controversial subject.

Globalization Is Good for Americans

"America and other wealthy countries have plainly gained *in* the aggregate from what is going on."

Clive Crook

In the following viewpoint, Clive Crook argues that globalization has been a positive development worldwide. The opening up of global markets has resulted in rapid growth of the global labor force. This growth has clearly been beneficial to developing countries, Crook argues. Furthermore, he says that despite the rhetoric, globalization is good for America and other rich countries, with workers continuing to see gains despite the growth in the overseas labor force. Crook is a senior editor of the *Atlantic Monthly*, a columnist for *National Journal*, and a commentator for the *Financial Times*.

AS YOU READ, CONSIDER THE FOLLOWING QUESTIONS:

1. According to Crook, how much has the global labor force expanded since 1980?
2. What is causing the gap between manufacturing wages in the United States and poor nations to shrink, according to the author?
3. According to Crook, real compensation for the average American worker has risen by how much since 1980?

Clive Crook, "Mistaking a Miracle for a Crisis," *National Journal*, vol. 39, April 14, 2007, pp. 12–13.
Reproduced with permission from *National Journal*, April 14, 2007. Copyright © 2009 by National
Journal Group, Inc. All rights reserved..

S uppose that America's labor force suddenly quadrupled. Imagine what that would do to unemployment. How would it be possible to find jobs for all of those people? Think of what it would mean for wages. How would we cope?

We are living through a transformation of just that sort in the world economy. Thanks to the opening of China, India, and Eastern Europe, and to breakthroughs in the technology of international trade, computing, and telecommunications, the internationally engaged global labor force has expanded fourfold since 1980—and most of that increase has happened, in fact, in just the past 15 years. We are in the midst of a great revolution in the way that people interact with one another, as producers and consumers, all around the planet.

To say this, of course, is commonplace: I am not claiming that the phenomenon has been ignored. On the contrary, the debate over how to manage this upheaval has become a driver of national politics in the United States. Despite their familiarity, however, the main facts about globalization, and their full implications, are not well understood. You could sum it up this way: The significance of this transformation is at the same time greatly overrated and greatly underrated.

FAST FACT

The World Bank estimates that full liberalization of global merchandise trade could, by 2015, increase revenues by $201 billion in high-income countries worldwide.

In the United States, as in every other advanced economy, voters and politicians are preoccupied with the national aspects. Are imports driving down our wages and putting Americans out of work? How far might offshoring of manufacturing and services go? What will that mean for us? But globalization is, self-evidently, an international event. What happens in any single country is just one highly connected aspect of what is happening somewhere else. What is happening (or thought to be happening) in individual countries has to add up to the big picture, taking the world as a whole, or else one has failed to grasp what is going on.

And when you look at the global context and try to do this adding up, the results are jarring. The global transition really is an awesome

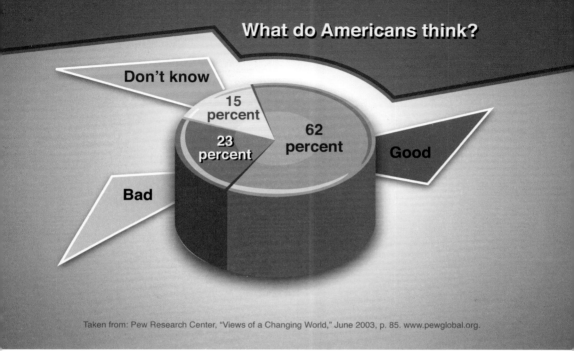

The Effects of Globalization on the United States

What do Americans think?

Don't know
15 percent

62 percent — Good

23 percent — Bad

Taken from: Pew Research Center, "Views of a Changing World," June 2003, p. 85. www.pewglobal.org.

shift in economic realities—colossal in scale and bewilderingly fast. Yet, seen in this light, the experiences of individual advanced economies, including that of the United States, seem quite muted. When you contemplate the pace and scale of the global transformation, it seems remarkable that economic life in America and Europe has not been much more dramatically recast.

The surprising thing is that the rich West is coping so easily and so well. America and other wealthy countries have plainly *gained* in the aggregate from what is going on—and the United States, in fact, has gained more than most. There are political strains, to be sure, but you could not call them unmanageable. Economic issues will be important in the elections of 2008, as they always are, but (so far as one can judge right now) not paramount. That such an enormous and sudden global upheaval can produce, country by country, such comparatively mild and, on the whole, beneficial results surely comes as a bit of a shock.

To get a better sense of both sides of this—the amazing drama of the global transformation and the comparative ease (automatic and unplanned, for the most part) with which the advanced economies have adapted to it—I have some reading to recommend. Don't be put off by the source. Twice a year the International Monetary Fund releases its *World Economic Outlook*. Because it includes some authoritative global economic forecasts, this is always essential reading for professional and amateur economists, but the newest edition, just out, contains a special chapter (www.imf.org/external/pubs/ft/weo/2007/01/pdf/c5.pdf) that deserves a much wider readership, especially among politicians and the people who work with them. This chapter, "The Globalization of Labor," weighs the implications of the new global economy for workers worldwide. It asks what exactly is going on, which groups are gaining or losing, and what governments might do to protect the victims. The study's global perspective is unusual and especially valuable, for the reason I just mentioned: It forces you to compare the pattern of change in the world as a whole with the effects that Americans are seeing at home.

A good way to gauge the scale of events from a high altitude is to think of globalization—shorthand for the opening up and interconnecting of local and national markets—as an increase in the worldwide supply of labor. The IMF's economists estimate it by weighting each country's labor supply based on the ratio of its exports to its gross domestic product. (So, for instance, if a country had no exports, it would be regarded as contributing nothing to the global labor supply; if its exports accounted for all of its GDP, then all of its workers would be deemed part of the global labor force.) By this measure, the global labor force grew fourfold—fourfold!—between 1980 and 2005, with a marked acceleration after 1990. How? The number of working-age people around the world grew, but that was not the main cause: That rise was only a little more than 50 percent. Most of the increase reflects the surge in exports—in international trade generally—that served to draw vast numbers of new workers into the global labor pool.

For workers in poor countries, this has been unambiguously good news. The IMF's numbers show that manufacturing wages in poor nations are rising—and quickly enough, overall, to shrink the gap with manufacturing wages in the United States. For the developing world's earliest industrializers, the gap has all but disappeared. In 1970, the average manufacturing wage in South Korea was less than 10 percent of the average manufacturing wage in America; by the turn of the century it was 70 percent. Wages in China, India, and other developing countries have so far converged with rich-world wages much more slowly than that—but the gap is closing nonetheless, and in most cases at an accelerating rate. Be clear about one thing: If you are interested in helping the world's poorest, globalization is the best possible news.

The International Monetary Fund says the global workforce grew fourfold between 1980 and 2005 and reflects a surge in global trade.

But what about workers in America and other rich countries? Given this huge expansion in the global labor force, you might expect a collapse in wages in America and Europe. Well, that has not happened. True, labor's share of national income has fallen in the United States and in other rich countries. In industries using mostly unskilled workers, labor's share of income has fallen significantly; in industries using mostly skilled labor, its share has tended to rise. But, thanks to trade, which has made prices lower than they otherwise would be, pay in real terms has kept on rising regardless—albeit more slowly in some places than in others. In America, real compensation per worker has risen by about 20 percent since 1980. In Europe, it has risen by more than 30 percent. (Note, though, that America has added new jobs at roughly twice Europe's rate—hence its consistently lower unemployment rate.)

Yes, growth in American wages and benefits was lower at that rate than the country had grown accustomed to. But see this in the global context: Despite the staggering increase in the effective global labor supply during the past two and a half decades—a phenomenon that is off all the charts and that, to repeat, heralds unprecedented inroads against global poverty—wages and benefits in the United States managed to keep on rising. This seems little short of miraculous.

How was it possible? Aside from the effect of trade on prices, the most important cause is the simplest, and yet the most frequently ignored. In their trade with other countries, developing nations do not confine themselves to selling goods and services; they also buy them. As they get richer, they import more, and that helps buoy incomes in the advanced economies. The IMF's figures show that since 1980, poor countries have increased their imports much faster than the advanced economies have increased theirs. And the share of industrial-country exports going to developing countries (rather than to other industrial countries) has been rising. Trade is a win-win proposition because, in the aggregate, it is a two-way process. Even so, it is remarkably good news that so much new labor has been absorbed so quickly into the global market system—and all, up to now, with so little disruption; indeed, it is happening alongside a continuing (albeit slow) rise in advanced-economy living standards.

None of this is to argue against measures that would help cushion the blow for those suffering the consequences of expanded international trade or technological change, or for others left behind. But it surely argues for shifting the focus of attention toward directly supporting the incomes of the low-paid, improving their skills, and providing better insurance against economic insecurity—and away from the generalized aversion to trade and globalization that continues to bubble up.

EVALUATING THE AUTHOR'S ARGUMENTS:

Crook explains that although wages in America have continued to rise with globalization, per capita income in jobs involving unskilled labor has not fared as well as in those involving skilled labor. Do you think the wages for unskilled labor are as important as for skilled labor? What, if any, are some benefits and drawbacks of low wages for unskilled labor?

Globalization Is Not Good for Most Americans

Mark Weisbrot

"The U.S. economy during a period in which it was mostly a closed economy (1946–1973) vastly outperformed the increasingly open economy."

In the following viewpoint Mark Weisbrot argues that the gains of globalization have been overstated. Weisbrot claims that despite contradictory claims made elsewhere, when all data are taken into account, productivity has not grown as much as it would have if globalization had not occurred. Furthermore, he believes that the vast majority of American workers have likely suffered an overall setback from globalization. Weisbrot is codirector of the Center for Economic and Policy Research in Washington, D.C., and president of Just Foreign Policy, an organization dedicated to reforming U.S. foreign policy. He is a columnist on economic and policy issues and is coauthor, with Dean Baker, of *Social Security: The Phony Crisis*.

AS YOU READ, CONSIDER THE FOLLOWING QUESTIONS:

1. By what percentage would productivity have grown since 1973 without globalization, according to the author?

2. According to Weisbrot, how have low- and middle-income countries fared over the last quarter century?
3. What does the author claim is responsible for the recent concern among economists about globalization?

In "A New Deal for Globalization," (*Foreign Affairs* July/August 2007), Kenneth Scheve and Matthew Slaughter have made a contribution by recognizing that what they call "a protectionist drift in public policy" in the U.S. is a result of the fact that the majority of the U.S. labor force has seen little (in recent decades) or no (in the last five years) income gains. They even acknowledge that "it is plausible that there is a connection" between the "skewed pattern of income growth" in the United States and globalization, something that most of the economics profession is still in denial about.

The New Open Economy

But the public's—and their elected representatives'—increasing rejection of "free trade" agreements has even more solid ground than the terrain that they depict. First, there is no need to exaggerate the potential gains from further reduction of the United States' relatively small remaining barriers to trade. For example, the authors state that an agreement in the Doha Round [the 2001 declaration that is aimed at lowering trade barriers around the world] of the WTO [World Trade Organization] negotiations would generate $500 billion per year in additional income in the United States. According to the World Bank's most recent estimates of various Doha Round scenarios, the United States would add between 0.02 and 0.05 percent to our annual GDP [gross domestic product], or between $2.7 and $6.8 billion a year, from a Doha agreement.

The authors also use productivity data for the U.S. to argue that "International trade and investment have spurred productivity growth" in the United States, noting that "the rate of increase in output per worker hour in the U.S. nonfarm business sector has doubled in the past decade, from an annual average of 1.35 percent between 1973 and 1995 to an annual average of 2.7 percent since 1995." If international trade and investment had really caused this magnitude of a productivity increase, this would be a powerful argument for such liberalization. However this does not appear to be the case. First, if we take a more comprehensive, economy-wide, and appropriate measure of usable productivity—taking into account such things as increased depreciation that counts as part of output but does not contribute to living standards—the picture is much different. By this measure, the annual rate of productivity growth increased by 0.9 percentage points in the years from 1995 to 2006 compared with the long 1973-1995 slowdown. Furthermore, productivity growth has slowed sharply over the last three years [2004–2007], raising the possibility that this decade-long uptick was just a one-time burst with no obvious connection to a quarter century of globalization.

Much more importantly, if we take a longer time period of accelerated international trade and investment liberalization, the picture is completely reversed. For example, we can ask the question, how much usable productivity growth would we have had since 1973, if we had experienced the same rate of usable productivity growth as occurred from 1946-1973? The answer is, productivity would have grown by 169.5 percent since 1973, as compared to its actual growth of 47.8 percent.

In other words, even ignoring the re-distribution of income in the last few decades, the U.S. economy during a period in which it was mostly a closed economy (1946–1973) vastly outperformed the increasingly open economy that we have had over the last 33 years, in terms of raising living standards.

An Economic Slowdown

Thus the authors' statement that "the integration of the world economy has boosted productivity and wealth creation in the United States and much of the rest of the world" is an assertion that remains to be demonstrated, and which does not find much support in the data. In fact, the vast majority of low- and middle-income countries have

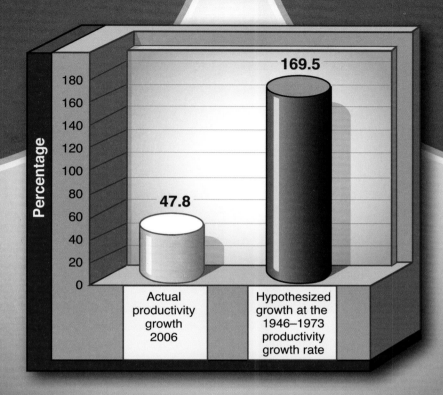

Productivity Growth in the United States

169.5

47.8

Percentage

180
160
140
120
100
80
60
40
20
0

| Actual productivity growth 2006 | Hypothesized growth at the 1946–1973 productivity growth rate |

Taken from: Dean Baker, "The Productivity to Paycheck Gap: What the Data Show," Center for Economic and Policy Research, April 2007. www.cepr.net.

suffered a sharp slowdown in economic growth and reduced progress on social indicators such as infant and child mortality, and life expectancy, over the last quarter century. This long-term economic slowdown is one of the main reasons that the Doha Round of the WTO is collapsing, and hemispheric agreements such as the proposed Free Trade Area of the Americas [a proposal that would eliminate or reduce trade barriers among all countries in the Americas, except Cuba] have been buried, after more than a decade of negotiations. There are important exceptions such as China that have indeed benefited from increased economic integration, but they did not follow the rules embodied in the WTO or other proposed commercial agreements.

The viewpoint's author points out that globalization has allowed Chinese manufacturers to benefit from global economic integration because they ignore the rules of the World Trade Organization.

In the United States, it is quite likely that the vast majority of the labor force has actually lost more from the redistribution of income and lowering of their real wages due to trade and investment liberalization, than they have gained from access to cheaper consumer goods. Ironically, now that outsourcing threatens to lower the incomes of professionals earning six-figure salaries, some economists have become concerned about globalization. But the gains from introduction of international competition to the protected professions such as law and medicine are many times greater than what the WTO could deliver in other goods and services.

This drives home the nature of what we are dealing with: it is not a question of "saving globalization" from "special-interest protectionists" as the authors argue. The "special interest protectionists"—highly paid professions, CEOs [chief executive officers], pharmaceutical companies and other monopolists—have been reaping the gains from misnamed "free-trade" agreements for many years, while subjecting the majority of Americans to international competition that has lowered their living standards. The "dangerous path" ahead is not so much the "creeping protectionism" feared by the authors as it is the continued use of global commercial agreements to increase income disparities in the United States.

EVALUATING THE AUTHORS' ARGUMENTS:

In this viewpoint Weisbrot concludes that the vast majority of the U.S. labor force has likely suffered a lowering of real compensation as a result of globalization. How does Weisbrot's claim here differ from Crook's claim in the previous viewpoint that overall compensation has risen?

Offshoring Jobs Does Not Harm American Workers

Robert Samuelson

"It's clear that globalization hasn't crippled the U.S. job machine."

In the following viewpoint Robert Samuelson argues that worries about offshoring have failed to be borne out. Citing a recent study, he claims that jobs lost to overseas outsourcing have been minimal. The vast majority of jobs lost, he argues, have domestic causes. He states that offshoring is not as easy as some claim and that it will continue to be less attractive as globalization evolves, putting to rest this particular concern about globalization. Samuelson writes on social, political, and economic issues as a weekly columnist for the *Washington Post* and a columnist for *Newsweek*. He is the author of *Untruth: Why the Conventional Wisdom Is (Almost Always) Wrong*.

AS YOU READ, CONSIDER THE FOLLOWING QUESTIONS:

1. How many jobs were lost in 2004 and 2005 to offshoring, according to Samuelson?

2. What three problems does Samuelson identify that make off-shoring difficult?
3. What will make offshoring less cost-competitive in the future, according to the author?

Remember the great "offshoring" debate? It was all the rage a few years ago.

Modern communications allowed white-collar work to be zapped around the world. We faced a terrifying future of hordes of well-educated and poorly paid Indians and Chinese stealing the jobs of middle-class engineers, accountants and software programmers in the U.S. and other wealthy nations. Merciless multinational companies would find the cheapest labor and to heck with all the lives ruined in the process.

What happened? Well, not much.

The Facts About Offshoring

Every so often, it's worth revisiting old controversies to see if the reality matches the rhetoric. In a recent paper, Jacob Funk Kirkegaard of the Peterson Institute for International Economics has done just that for offshoring (aka overseas "outsourcing"). He reviewed many studies. His conclusion: "The heated public and political debate has been vastly overblown."

For the U.S., Kirkegaard examined a survey on "mass layoffs" from the Bureau of Labor Statistics [BLS] to see how many stemmed from offshoring. Answer: 4%. That included both manufacturing and service jobs.

In 2004 and 2005, the BLS counted almost 1 million workers fired in layoffs of 50 or more. That itself isn't a huge number in a labor force of about 150 million.

Moreover, most causes were domestic. The largest reason (accounting for about 25%) was "contract completion"—a public works job done, a movie finished. Other big categories included "downsizing" (16%) and the combination of bankruptcy and "financial difficulty" (10%). Only about 12% of layoffs stemmed from "movement of work"—a category that would include offshoring. But two-thirds of the moves were domestic.

Job Relocations Within the United States and to International Locations Lead to Mass Layoffs

Some job losses in the United States occur due to movement of work to overseas locations both within and outside companies (offshoring), but many more are lost due to the relocation of work domestically.

Domestic job losses in the United States occur because of

- changes in internal company structure.
- movement of jobs to other company work sites.
- movement of work to a producer not affiliated with the company.

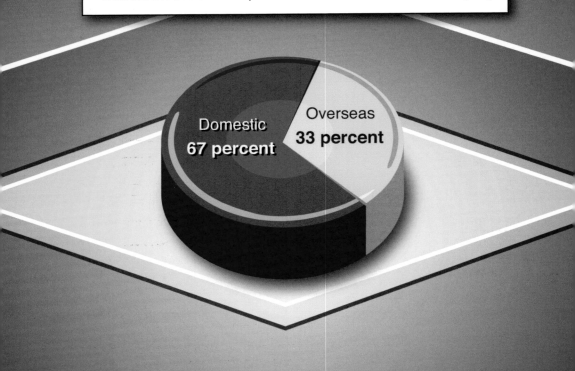

Domestic
67 percent

Overseas
33 percent

Taken from: Jacob Funk Kirkegaard, "Offshoring, Outsourcing, and Production Relocation—Labor-Market Effects in the OECD Countries and Developing Asia," Peter G. Peterson Institute for International Economics, April 2007, p. 39./S.P. Brown, *Mass Layoff Statistics in the United States and Domestic and Overseas Relocation*, Washington, DC: Bureau of Labor Statistics, 2004.

Kirkegaard located a similar survey for Europe. Although the cutoff for layoffs was higher (100 workers), the results were similar. About 5% of job losses resulted from offshoring. The other 95% involved bankruptcies, "downsizing," domestic outsourcing and firings after mergers.

Among wealthy nations, Japan was the only major example of a possibly larger effect. It may have lost factory jobs to China. From 2001 to 2006, Japanese manufacturing employment dropped by 1.3 million, to 11.5 million; meanwhile, jobs at Japanese manufacturing affiliates abroad rose by 900,000. But Kirkegaard thinks Japan's loss of manufacturing jobs could also have resulted from greater productivity.

Offshoring Is Not Easy

It's true that offshoring doesn't measure the full impact of globalization on U.S. labor markets. That effect would also include trade and investment by multinational firms. Still, with the unemployment rate at 4.5% [in 2007], it's clear that globalization hasn't crippled the U.S. job machine.

> **FAST FACT**
>
> A Reason Foundation report claims that between 1996 and 2003, offshore outsourcing was responsible for just 0.9 percent of the jobs lost in mass layoffs in the United States.

One reason for modest offshoring is that it's not so easy to do. It involves more than just changing phone numbers and switching computer hookups. A survey by the consulting firm A.T. Kearney found the following problems: cross-border differences of culture and language (80%); lack of skills offshore (49%); customer complaints (49%).

As communications technology improves—and companies gain experience—offshoring may increase. Some economists still expect it to explode. Writing in the *Washington Post*, Alan Blinder of Princeton said "offshoring may be the biggest political issue in economics for a generation," threatening "tens of millions of American workers."

Indeed, some studies examined by Kirkegaard estimated that a fifth of U.S. jobs could theoretically be moved abroad. But just because a job can theoretically be relocated doesn't mean that it will.

Between 2001and 2006 Japan's domestic manufacturing employment dropped by 1.3 million, while manufacturing jobs at the country's affiliates abroad increased by 900,000.

Adjustments occur. Developing countries need skilled workers for their own economies, not just exports. India's entire information technology industry employs less than 1% of the nation's work force.

As the global demand for services—engineering, programming—rises, so will the wages of foreign service workers (engineers, programmers, accountants). That will make offshoring less cost-competitive.

Finally, if countries run big trade surpluses from offshoring, their currencies should rise. That, too, would reduce their cost advantage (and it explains why changing China's artificially undervalued exchange rate is important).

The Causes of Job Losses

Losing a job is a wrenching experience for anyone, but the lesson here is that most job losses have local causes. The offshoring obsession reflects its novelty and the potential threat to white-collar jobs that seemed inherently safe from foreign competition.

In our mind's eye, globalization is so powerful it's sweeping everything before it. The reality is that, though globalization is increasingly important, it's still a weakling compared with the domestic economy. The antidote to job loss is job creation, and that depends decisively on national economic policies and conditions.

It's easy to blame all our economic anxieties and problems on globalization, because that makes foreigners and multinational companies responsible. Though satisfying, it will also be self-defeating if it diverts attention from fostering a healthy economy at home.

EVALUATING THE AUTHOR'S ARGUMENTS:

Samuelson claims that the number of jobs lost to offshoring has not been as significant as anticipated. Make a list of the sources Samuelson uses to back up his claim.

Offshoring Jobs Harms American Workers

Alan S. Blinder

"Even if we do everything I've suggested . . . American workers will still face a troublesome transition as tens of millions of old jobs are replaced by new ones."

In the following viewpoint Alan S. Blinder argues that the offshoring of jobs caused by globalization will continue to be painful for American workers for a long time. He argues that two historical forces will continue to increase the problem of lost jobs domestically for the foreseeable future. Blinder is the Gordon S. Rentschler Memorial Professor of Economics and Public Affairs at Princeton University and codirector of Princeton's Center for Economic Policy Studies. He is also vice chairman of the Promontory Interfinancial Network. Blinder is coauthor, with Jagdish N. Bhagwati, of the book, *Offshoring of American Jobs: What Response from U.S. Economic Policy?*

AS YOU READ, CONSIDER THE FOLLOWING QUESTIONS:

1. In what way does Blinder argue that the nature of international trade is changing?

2. What two forces does Blinder believe are going to make the transition of American workers large, lengthy, and painful?
3. Approximately how many jobs does Blinder argue are potentially offshorable?

I'm a free trader down to my toes. Always have been. Yet lately, I'm being treated as a heretic by many of my fellow economists. Why? Because I have stuck my neck out and predicted that the offshoring of service jobs from rich countries such as the United States to poor countries such as India may pose major problems for tens of millions of American workers over the coming decades. In fact, I think offshoring may be the biggest political issue in economics for a generation.

Trade Is Changing

When I say this, many of my fellow free-traders react with a mixture of disbelief, pity and hostility. Blinder, have you lost your mind? (Answer: I think not.) Have you forgotten about the basic economic gains from international trade? (Answer: *No*.) Are you advocating some form of protectionism? (Answer: *No!*) Aren't you giving aid and comfort to the enemies of free trade? (Answer: No, I'm trying to save free trade from itself.)

The reason for my alleged apostasy [defection] is that the nature of international trade is changing before our eyes. We used to think, roughly, that an item was tradable only if it could be put in a box and shipped. That's no longer true. Nowadays, a growing list of services can be zapped across international borders electronically. It's electrons that move, not boxes. We're all familiar with call centers, but electronic service delivery has already extended to computer programming, a variety of engineering services, accounting, security analysis and a lot else. And much more is on the way.

Why do I say much more? Because two powerful, historical forces are driving these changes, and both are virtually certain to grow stronger over time.

Two Historical Forces

The first is technology, especially information and communications technology, which has been improving at an astonishing pace in recent decades. As the technology advances, the quality of now-familiar modes of communication (such as telephones, videoconferencing and the Internet) will improve, and entirely new forms of communication may be invented. One clear implication of the upward march of technology is that a widening array of services will become deliverable electronically from afar. And it's not just low-skill services such as key punching, transcription and telemarketing. It's also high-skill services such as radiology, architecture and engineering—maybe even college teaching.

The second driver is the entry of about 1.5 billion "new" workers into the world economy. These folks aren't new to the world, of course. But they live in places such as China, India and the former Soviet bloc—countries that used to stand outside the world economy. For those who say, "Sure, but most of them are low-skilled workers," I

New communications technologies such as videoconferencing allow services to be delivered electronically from afar and may adversely affect American job seekers.

have two answers. First, even a small percentage of 1.5 billion people is a lot of folks. And second, India and China will certainly educate hundreds of millions more in the coming decades. So there will be a lot of willing and able people available to do the jobs that technology will move offshore.

The Global and National Effects

Looking at these two historic forces from the perspective of the world as a whole, one can only get a warm feeling. Improvements in technology will raise living standards, just as they have since the dawn of the Industrial Revolution. And the availability of millions of new electronically deliverable service jobs in, say, India and China will help alleviate poverty on a mass scale. Offshoring will also reduce costs and boost productivity in the United States. So repeat after me: Globalization is good for the world. Which is where economists usually stop.

And where my alleged apostasy starts.

FAST FACT

A recent poll surveyed Americans' views toward the term "outsourcing" and found that 22 percent felt positive about the term; 63 percent were negative toward it.

For these same forces don't look so benign from the viewpoint of an American computer programmer or accountant. They've done what they were told to do: They went to college and prepared for well-paid careers with bountiful employment opportunities. But now their bosses are eyeing legions of well-qualified, English-speaking programmers and accountants in India, for example, who will happily work for a fraction of what Americans earn. Such prospective competition puts a damper on wage increases. And if the jobs do move offshore, displaced American workers may lose not only their jobs but also their pensions and health insurance. These people can be forgiven if they have doubts about the virtues of globalization.

We economists assure folks that things will be all right in the end. Both Americans and Indians will be better off. I think that's right. The basic principles of free trade that [economists] Adam Smith and

David Ricardo taught us two centuries ago remain valid today: Just like people, nations benefit by specializing in the tasks they do best and trading with other nations for the rest. There's nothing new here theoretically.

A Lengthy and Painful Transition

But I would argue that there's something new about the coming transition to service offshoring. Those two powerful forces mentioned earlier—technological advancement and the rise of China and India—suggest that this particular transition will be large, lengthy and painful.

It's going to be lengthy because the technology for moving information across the world will continue to improve for decades, if not forever. So, for those who earn their living performing tasks that are (or will become) deliverable electronically, this is no fleeting problem.

It's also going to be large. How large? In some recent research, I estimated that 30 million to 40 million U.S. jobs are potentially offshorable. These include scientists, mathematicians and editors on

The Four Main Offshoring Occupational Categories

Category	Description	Number of Occupations	Number of Workers (millions)
I	Highly offshorable	59	8.2
II	Offshorable	151	20.7
III	Non-offshorable	74	8.8
IV	Highly non-offshorable	533	92.6
All		817	130.3

Taken from: Alan S. Blinder, "How Many U.S. Jobs Might Be Offshorable?" CEPS Working Paper No. 142, Center for Economic Policy Studies, March 2007.

the high end and telephone operators, clerks and typists on the low end. Obviously, not all of these jobs are going to India, China or elsewhere. But many will.

It's going to be painful because our country offers such a poor social safety net to cushion the blow for displaced workers. Our unemployment insurance program is stingy by first-world standards. American workers who lose their jobs often lose their health insurance and pension rights as well. And even though many displaced workers will have to change occupations—a difficult task for anyone—only a fortunate few will be offered opportunities for retraining. All this needs to change.

Some Solutions

What else is to be done? Trade protection won't work. You can't block electrons from crossing national borders. Because U.S. labor cannot compete on price, we must reemphasize the things that have kept us on top of the economic food chain for so long: technology, innovation, entrepreneurship, adaptability and the like. That means more science and engineering, more spending on R&D [research and development], keeping our capital markets big and vibrant, and not letting ourselves get locked into "sunset" industries.

In addition, we need to rethink our education system so that it turns out more people who are trained for the jobs that will remain in the United States and fewer for the jobs that will migrate overseas. We cannot, of course, foresee exactly which jobs will go and which will stay. But one good bet is that many electronic service jobs will move offshore, whereas personal service jobs will not. Here are a few examples. Tax accounting is easily offshorable; onsite auditing is not. Computer programming is offshorable; computer repair is not. Architects could be endangered, but builders aren't. Were it not for stiff regulations, radiology would be offshorable; but pediatrics and geriatrics aren't. Lawyers who write contracts can do so at a distance and deliver them electronically; litigators who argue cases in court cannot.

But even if we do everything I've suggested—which we won't— American workers will still face a troublesome transition as tens of millions of old jobs are replaced by new ones. There will also be great political strains on the open trading system as millions of white-collar workers who thought their jobs were immune to foreign competition suddenly find that the game has changed—and not to their liking.

That is why I am going public with my concerns now. If we economists stubbornly insist on chanting "Free trade is good for you" to people who know that it is not, we will quickly become irrelevant to the public debate. Compared with that, a little apostasy should be welcome.

EVALUATING THE AUTHORS' ARGUMENTS:

In the previous viewpoint Robert Samuelson argues that the concerns about offshoring are not as great as anticipated, partly due to the difficulty of offshoring jobs. How might the two historical forces that Blinder mentions decrease the difficulty of offshoring jobs in the future?

America's Trade Deficit Is Not a Problem

David Malpass

"The trade deficit and related capital inflow reflect U.S. growth, not weakness."

In the following viewpoint David Malpass argues that America's trade deficit—importing more than is exported—signals economic strength, not weakness. Malpass cites various economic data in support of his view that despite having a trade deficit for several years, the U.S. economy is strong. He believes that one of the reasons for the deficit is the particular demographics of the United States in comparison to other countries. Rather than trying to eliminate the trade deficit, Malpass believes that the United States should rely on its shifting demographics and growth to keep the economy strong. Malpass, former chief economist of Bear Stearns, is president of Encima Global, a global economic research firm.

AS YOU READ, CONSIDER THE FOLLOWING QUESTIONS:

1. According to Malpass, how many jobs were created in the United States between 2001 and 2006, despite the trade surplus?

David Malpass, "Embrace the (Trade) Deficit," *The Wall Street Journal,* December 21, 2006, p. A16. Reproduced by permission of the author.

For decades, the trade deficit has been a political and journalistic lightning rod, inspiring countless predictions of America's imminent economic collapse. The reality is different. Our imports grow with our economy and population while our exports grow with foreign economies, especially those of industrialized countries. Though widely criticized as an imbalance, the trade deficit and related capital inflow reflect U.S. growth, not weakness—they link the younger, faster-growing U.S. with aging, slower-growing economies abroad.

Key Data

Since the 2001 recession, the U.S. economy has created 9.3 million new jobs, compared with 360,000 in Japan and 1.1 million in the euro zone excluding Spain. This despite our trade deficit and their trade surpluses. Like the U.S., Spain (3.6 million new jobs) and the U.K. (1.3 million new jobs) ran trade deficits and created jobs rapidly in this five-year period. Wages are rising solidly in these three. The economics is clear (for once) that a liberal trading environment allows more jobs with higher wages as people specialize.

The latest data [as of December 2006] on growth in jobs, retail sales and housing starts, and the record level of household savings, underscores the solid economy described by Fed [Federal Reserve] Chairman Ben Bernanke last month [November 2006]. Supporting the "solid-growth" view are rising global stock markets, strong growth of corporate profits, the narrow credit spread between Treasurys and riskier bonds, and low interest rates relative to inflation and to growth—nominal growth in the 12 months through September was 6%, yet the Fed funds rate, usually in line with nominal growth, only averaged 4.6%.

The trade deficit and a low "personal savings rate" are key parts of the bond market's multi-year pessimism about the U.S. growth outlook. But just as the high level of U.S. savings is likely to add to

A Favorable Trade Imbalance

- The **balance of trade** is the value of the exports of a given country—in this case, the United States—minus the value of its imports. The trade balance is the difference between these two values.

- A **capital account surplus** (trade surplus) occurs when a country sells more goods and services to other countries than it buys from them.

- A **current account deficit** (trade deficit) occurs when the United States, or any country, buys more goods and services from other countries than it sells to them.

  Foreign countries may take a portion of what the U.S. pays them for goods and services and reinvest it in the United States, improving the U.S. economy. Some experts say such investments mean that the U.S. trade deficit is actually a sign of U.S. economic growth, rather than weakness.

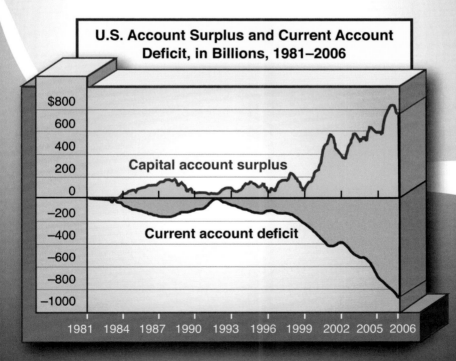

U.S. Account Surplus and Current Account Deficit, in Billions, 1981–2006

Capital account surplus

Current account deficit

Taken from: David Malpass, "Embrace the Deficit," *Wall Street Journal*, December 21, 2006, p. A16./Haver Analytics.

future growth—the savings rate is only low if you arbitrarily exclude gains—the trade deficit and heavy capital inflows are also positive parts of the growth outlook. Rather than signaling a slowdown, the inversion of the yield curve—"Greenspan's conundrum," in which bond yields are low despite solid growth and rising inflation—is probably the result of this deep underestimate of the U.S. growth outlook, plentiful liquidity, and a backward-looking deflation premium for bonds, the reverse of the backward-looking inflation premium that kept bond yields unusually high in the 1980s.

FAST FACT

According to the U.S. Census Bureau, in 2008 the U.S. trade deficit was $677 billion, with imports totaling $2,520 billion and exports totaling $1,843 billion.

The Reason for the Deficit

The common perception is that Americans drive the trade deficit in an unhealthy way by spending more than we produce. To make up the difference, foreigners ship us things on credit. This sounds bad, but should be evaluated in terms of our demographics, low unemployment rate, attractiveness to foreign investment and rising household savings.

The recent surge in the U.S. trade deficit reflects, in part, the unprecedented shift in the demographics of the world's large economies. The under-60 U.S. population is expected to grow for at least 50 years while the under-60 populations in Japan and Europe are already declining and in China will turn down within a decade. They need bonds while Americans need capital. They want to save more than they invest in their own economies, and are eager to help us invest more heavily (through their purchase of bonds). This makes good demographic sense. Older investors (concentrated abroad) need steady returns, lending to younger generations through bank deposits, bond purchases and life insurance premiums (which are reinvested in growth). Younger people (concentrated in the U.S.) need cash and debt for college degrees, houses and business startups. This creates a healthy synergy across generations and across borders.

Like young households, many companies also spend more than they produce, using bonds and bank loans, some from foreigners, to make up the difference. They add employees, machines, supplies and advertising before they produce. Growing corporations are expected to be cash hungry. This leverage is treated as a positive for companies but a negative for countries, a key inconsistency in popular economics. Rather than paying the debt back, the growing company rolls the debt over and adds more, just as the U.S. has been doing throughout most of its prosperous economic history. Part of each additional bond offering puts the company and the U.S. in the position of investing more than we save, drawing in foreign investment and contributing to the trade deficit.

With all the negativism about the U.S. economy, it's easy to forget its attractiveness. Foreigners are as eager to invest in the U.S. as we are to buy goods and services from them—it's a two-way street. Our 10-year government bonds yield 4.6% per year versus 1.6% in Japan, while our government debt is 38% of GDP [gross domestic

The author says that the recent surge in the U.S. trade deficit is due in part to a shift in demographics. In the United States the under-sixty population is expected to grow for the next fifty years.

product] versus 86% in Japan. The comparisons with Europe are not as extreme as Japan's, but still heavily favor the U.S.

While the net foreign debt of the U.S. is growing (the result of capital inflows), household net worth is growing faster, meaning foreigners are investing in the U.S. too slowly and conservatively to keep up with our growth. Their capital mingles with domestic savings, providing $2.7 trillion of net international capital to combine with $27 trillion in net U.S. household financial savings as of Sept. 30 [2006].

Relying on Growth and Demographics

The already-large foreign demand for investments in the U.S. is likely to grow from here, putting upward pressure on the trade deficit even if foreign growth continues to accelerate. The U.S. offers a relatively high and steady return on investment—high because of the innovation and growth taking place here, steady because the commodity and manufacturing parts of many businesses are increasingly done abroad, reducing the volatility in U.S. growth. Equally important, the demographics of the world's large economies are shifting rapidly in favor of the U.S.

The trade deficit is the mechanism allowing consumption and investment in the U.S. to grow faster than in Europe and Japan. The issue for the U.S. is whether it's worth the interest costs. It's the same question facing a small business: Should it borrow money to expand the payroll, train employees, buy land and machines, conduct R&D [research and development], build inventory? Profit and credit-worthiness help make the decision.

The post-election dollar weakness pleased those who still think the U.S. is heading in the wrong economic direction. They advocate a weaker dollar as medicine for the trade deficit, often blaming it for more economic problems than we actually have.

But the trade deficit, around for hundreds of years of solid American growth, doesn't justify the inflation risk from dollar weakness or the growth risk from protectionism. And the trade deficit probably wouldn't respond to a weaker dollar anyway—yen strength hasn't dented Japan's trade surplus, and it took a recession to create our last trade surplus in 1990–1991.

The swing vote on the dollar, and probably the controlling vote, is Fed policy. For now, this leaves unresolved the market debate over whether the U.S. will encourage dollar weakness and inflation in an effort to fight the trade deficit. More likely the Fed will fight inflation, strengthening the dollar, and leaving the trade deficit dependent on U.S. growth and demographics—right where it should be.

EVALUATING THE AUTHOR'S ARGUMENTS:

In this viewpoint Malpass argues against the perception that America's trade deficit, spending more than is produced, is unfavorable. Why do you think someone would take the opposite view and argue that a trade deficit is not good for America?

America's Trade Deficit Is a Problem

Jon Rynn

"In order to save globalization, the U.S. will have to lessen it."

In the following viewpoint Jon Rynn argues that the trade deficit in the United States is causing the value of the dollar to drop. Moreover, Rynn claims that the loss in the value of the dollar is not causing the expected result of more U.S. exports. He concludes that the only solution is to focus efforts domestically to eliminate the trade deficit. Rynn is a political science instructor who writes for the Global Makeover blog of the Economic Reconstruction Network, which advocates a progressive agenda, including an environmentally sustainable economic system.

AS YOU READ, CONSIDER THE FOLLOWING QUESTIONS:

1. According to Rynn, the trade deficit of the United States in 2007 was equal to what percent of the gross domestic product, or GDP?
2. As the author explains it, what happens to the cost of U.S. imports if the value of the dollar goes down?
3. What job sector does Rynn believe needs to be rebuilt in order to export more and import less?

The United States trade deficit is threatening to upend globalization as we've known it. The rise in the price of oil has been leading to a similar result: an international trading system in which there is much less trading. Now, that may actually be a good thing, in the long-run, but in the case of the United States it might happen in a very chaotic way.

This problem that has been accelerating since George W. Bush [U.S. president, January 2001 to January 2009] took office: The United States has been buying many more goods than it has been selling. As I hope to explain, eventually this will lead to a sharp fall in the value of the dollar, which will lead to a sharp fall in our standard of living.

The Problem with the Trade Deficit

If we have any hope of transforming our economy from one that is dependent on greenhouse gas–spewing fossil fuels, industrial agriculture, and inefficient transportation systems, then we will have to embark on a truly gargantuan building program in order to construct all of the wind turbines, solar panels, high-speed rail, light rail, electric cars, organic farms, and energy self-sufficient buildings that we can. In order to do that, however, we have to be wealthy. At the rate we're going, we won't be, and poor nations can't import lots of good stuff from abroad.

Allow me [to] explain why buying too much and selling too little could have such devastating effects:

Nations eventually get into big trouble when they import from other countries too much, and they sell too little. When this imbalance occurs, it's called a *trade deficit*. The U.S. trade deficit has been getting bigger and bigger for many years now. Last year [2007] it actually *improved* to $711 billion. Even though we exported $1,148 billion worth of goods and $479 billion worth of services, we imported $1,966 billion worth of goods (including $331 billion in oil) and $372 billion worth of services (all figures from the Bureau of Economic Analysis, part of the Department of Commerce). Since the total of all goods and services produced in the U.S. (GDP [gross domestic product]) in 2007 was $13,807.5 billion, that means that the trade deficit was equal to 5.1 percent of GDP.

The author argues that the U.S. manufacturing economy should be rebuilt through new green industries such as wind and solar power.

So, what's wrong with that? The problem is that the people selling us all of that stuff have $711 billion that they're stuck with. What do they do with the dollars? This has been going on for a while, so that there are now about $6,500 billion floating around the world because of our trade deficits.

According to *Economy in Crisis*, over $2,000 billion has been spent buying up the United States since 1978, while most of the extra dollars have been deposited in a variety of ways, with the interest being paid to foreign governments and companies. But that's not the worst of it. The worst is what is happening in slow motion: *The value of the dollar is collapsing.*

The Sinking Dollar

Why would that happen? Because people holding dollars can't buy what they want with the extra dollars, or can't buy as much as they used to. They may have bought most of the good things to buy in the United States. Another prop of the value of the dollar could be kicked away: The oil-producing countries accept only dollars for oil, and if the dollar keeps declining, they'll want to accept other currencies, meaning people will have even less reason to hang on to dollars.

Price is determined by supply and demand. If supply goes up and/or demand goes down, the price goes down. The demand for dollars is going down while the supply is going up. When the dollar becomes worth less, then the cost, in dollars, of the things we buy from abroad go up. Foreign goods and services become more expensive, there's inflation, we buy less.

It gets worse. What's supposed to happen next is what is *not* going to happen next: since the value of the dollar is sinking, the cost to foreigners of our goods and services will go down, making our goods more attractive, meaning that foreigners *should* buy more of

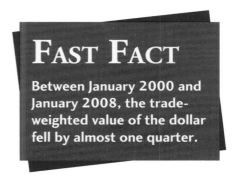

FAST FACT

Between January 2000 and January 2008, the trade-weighted value of the dollar fell by almost one quarter.

our goods, our exports *should* go up, the trade deficit *should* go down, bada bing, everything should be hunky-dory. And exports *have* been going up, except that according to *The New York Times*, the "Export boom helps farms, not American factories":

> But the world is not suddenly snapping up made-in-America goods like aircraft, machinery and staplers. The great attraction is decidedly low-luster commodities like corn, wheat, ore and scrap metal—while Boeing's aircraft or Caterpillar's tractors are distinctive and sought after, corn grown in Iowa is virtually interchangeable with corn grown in Argentina or any other breadbasket country. "Over a long period," Mr. [L. Josh] Bivens [of the Economic Policy Institute] said, "commodities contribute right around zero to export growth."

"US imports huge compared to US exports," cartoon by Dwane Powell. Used with permission of Dwane Powell and Creators Syndicate. All rights reserved.

This export boom is related to ethanol production, which is destroying the soil, and will lead to an impoverished agricultural system in the future—which means it can't last anyway.

Even though the dollar is going down, exports of manufactured goods are not going up. And why not? As the *New York Times* says:

> The manufacturers themselves acknowledge that they gradually undercut their ability to export as they moved more and more production to factories overseas. Bringing that production back to this country, so that it could be exported, would dismantle global networks constructed relentlessly over the last 25 years.

> "We have achieved a worldwide manufacturing base, and we are not going to shut down our factories overseas," said Franklin J. Vargo, vice president for international economics at the National Association of Manufacturers. "But on the margin, we will shift a little bit of manufacturing back to the United States."

Thanks a bunch, Vargo, for some marginal adjustments. Meanwhile, as the dollar falls, the only way for the trade deficit to close will be for the dollar to fall even *further* until foreign goods are so expensive, and we import so much less, that our imports equal our exports.

Import Less, Export More

What has this got to do with globalization? Since about $600 billion of that trade deficit comes from China, Europe, Japan, Mexico, and Canada, a slashing of trade would have a major effect on global trade patterns. China, in particular, has been unilaterally keeping its currency, the yuan, at too high a value; either they have to allow it to be valued by the global currency market, or the U.S. will be forced to unilaterally revalue the dollar (perhaps with tariffs).

The irony is this: in order to save globalization, the U.S. will have to lessen it. If the U.S. rebuilds its manufacturing sector so that it doesn't have to import as many goods and can export more goods, then the dollar will not collapse, and a healthy amount of trade—that is, trade that will be possible with expensive oil—can continue. But if the U.S. continues to hollow out its manufacturing base, eventually it will turn into the equivalent of a poor country, only able to sell raw materials to the richer countries that can manufacture.

Rebuilding the manufacturing economy by building up green industries like wind and solar equipment, rail, and electric cars is not only good for green collar job creation, but it will also allow us to balance our trade because we would not have to import oil and we could trade our manufactured goods for foreign manufactured goods.

Here's the political punchline: We can either have a green economy or a poor one.

EVALUATING THE AUTHORS' ARGUMENTS:

In this viewpoint Jon Rynn worries that the trade deficit will lead to a poor economy unless eliminated, whereas David Malpass, in the previous viewpoint, argues that the trade deficit is not a concern. What fundamental disagreement do Rynn and Malpass have about the relationship between a weak U.S. dollar and the trade deficit?

Chapter 2

Is Globalization Good for the World?

The good and bad effects of globalization on countries' economies is explored in this chapter.

Globalization Is Good for Countries Worldwide

Tyler Cowen

"The classic economic recipes of trade, investment and good incentives have never been more successful in generating huge gains in human welfare."

In the following viewpoint Tyler Cowen argues that the greatest benefit from globalization, including trade, is a rise in living standards around the world. Cowen claims that not only has globalization improved the lives of those in many developing countries, but Americans benefit from the opening of global markets. He believes that fears about globalization are misplaced and irrational. Cowen is a professor of economics at George Mason University and at the Center for the Study of Public Choice at George Mason University. He is the author of *Discover Your Inner Economist: Use Incentives to Fall in Love, Survive Your Next Meeting, and Motivate Your Dentist.*

AS YOU READ, CONSIDER THE FOLLOWING QUESTIONS:
1. What countries does the author identify as having improved their living standards over the last twenty years?
2. What does Cowen claim is the best benefit of globalized trade?
3. What does the author identify as the fear that is driving the backlash against globalization?

T he last 20 years have brought the world more trade, more globalization and more economic growth than in any previous such period in history. Few commentators had believed that such a rise in trade and living standards was possible so quickly.

Gains Worldwide

More than 400 million Chinese climbed out of poverty between 1990 and 2004, according to the World Bank. India has become a rapidly growing economy, the middle class in Brazil and Mexico is flourishing, and recent successes of Ghana and Tanzania show that parts of Africa may be turning the corner as well.

Despite these enormous advances, however, there is a backlash against globalization and a widespread belief that it requires moderation. Ordinary people often question the benefits of international trade, and now many intellectuals are turning more skeptical, too. Yet the facts on the ground show that the current climate of economic doom and gloom simply isn't warranted. The classic economic recipes of trade, investment and good incentives have never been more successful in generating huge gains in human welfare.

The globalization process has had its bumps, of course, as reflected recently by rising commodity prices, but that is largely a consequence of how much and how rapidly prosperity has grown. Countries like China have become richer so fast that global production of energy and food have been unable to match the pace. But rapid economic growth is the right direction, even if some of the remaining poor are suffering from high food prices.

The Benefit of New Ideas

For all the talk of a needed "timeout" from globalization, world trade is actually accelerating, and that is for the better. Big changes often come bunched together, so that when good things are happening it is important to maintain the trend. It's true that the tariff-reducing talks at the World Trade Organization have stalled and that the Democratic Party, at least in its rhetoric, has moved away from the free-trade legacy of President Bill Clinton.

But the volume of trade is nonetheless likely to keep rising, if only because the world economy is expanding. Furthermore, a vast major-

A man watches commodity stock prices at the Shanghai Stock Exchange in China. China's booming economy has caused a rise in commodity prices worldwide.

ity of Americans have never been better poised to benefit from global exchange and from the prosperity of the rest of the world.

Trade advocates focus on the benefits of goods arriving from abroad, like luxury shoes from Italy or computer chips from Taiwan. But new ideas are the real prize. By 2010, China will have more Ph.D. scientists and engineers than the United States. These professionals are not fundamentally a threat. To the contrary, they are creators, whose ideas are likely to improve the lives of ordinary Americans, not just the business elites. The more access the Chinese have to American and other markets, the more they can afford higher education and the greater their incentive to innovate.

Conservative and liberal economists agree that new ideas are the fundamental source of higher living standards. We urgently need new biotechnologies, a cure for AIDS and a cleaner energy infrastructure, to name just a few. Trade is part of the path toward achieving those ends. A wealthier China and India also mean higher potential rewards for Americans and others who invest in innovation. A product or idea that might have been marketed just to the United States and to Europe 20 years ago could be sold to billions more in the future.

Those benefits will take time to arrive, but trade with China has already eased hardships for poorer Americans. A new research paper by Christian Broda and John Romalis, both professors at the Graduate School of Business at the University of Chicago, has shown that cheap imports from China have benefited the American poor disproportionately. In fact, for the poor, discounting in stores such as Wal-Mart has offset much of the rise in measured income inequality from 1994 to 2005.

The Real Fear of Globalization

Despite all these gains, the prevailing intellectual tendency these days is to apologize for free trade. A common claim is that trade liberalization should proceed only if it is accompanied by new policies to retrain displaced workers or otherwise ameliorate the consequences of economic volatility.

Yes, the benefits of a good safety net are well established, but globalization is not the primary source of trouble for most American workers. Health care problems, bad schools for our children or, in recent times, bad banking practices have all produced greater disruptions—and these have been fundamentally domestic failings.

What's really happening is that many people, whether in the United States or abroad, are unduly suspicious about economic relations with foreigners. These complaints stem from basic human nature—namely, our tendency to divide people into "in groups" and "out groups" and to elevate one and to demonize the other. Americans fear that foreigners will rise at their expense or "control" some aspects of the economy.

One approach is to appease these sentiments by backing away from trade just a bit, or by managing it, so as to limit the backlash. Giving up momentum, however, isn't necessarily the right way forward. If we are too apologetic about globalization, we can feed core irrationalities, instead of taming them. The risk is that we will frame trade as a fundamental source of suffering and losses, which would make voters more nervous, not less.

It is wrong to play down the costs of globalization, but the reality is that we've been playing down its benefits for a long time. Politicians

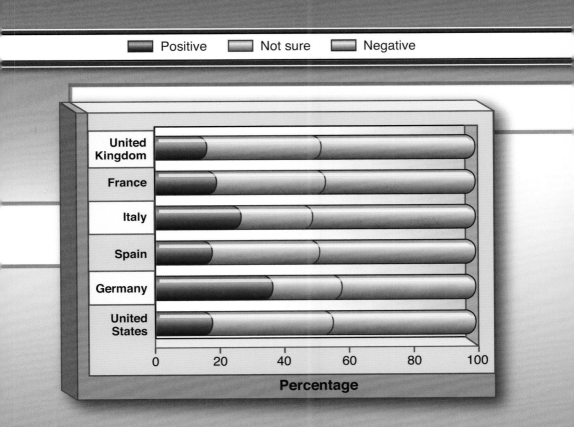

Globalization Backlash in Rich Nations

Do you think globalization is having a positive or negative effect in your country?

Positive   Not sure   Negative

Taken from: *Financial Times*/Harris Poll: Chris Giles, "Globalization Backlash in Rich Nations," *Financial Times*, July 27, 2007.

already pander to Americans' suspicion of foreigners. There is no need for the rest of us to jump on this bandwagon. Instead, we need more awareness of the cosmopolitan benefits of trade and the often hidden—but no less real—gains for ordinary Americans.

If we look at trends of the last 20 years, we have every reason to believe that the modern era of free trade is just getting started.

EVALUATING THE AUTHOR'S ARGUMENTS:

In this viewpoint Cowen claims that wealth in countries such as India and China leads to more wealth for Americans by providing a market for U.S. products in these countries. What is an example of an American product that might experience export growth as India and China get wealthier?

Globalization Is Not Good for Countries Worldwide

Julian Brookes, interviewing John Ralston Saul

"A small group of people are getting richer and a much larger group of people are getting poorer."

In the following viewpoint Julian Brookes interviews John Ralston Saul about Saul's view that globalization is not working. Brookes claims that globalization was the outgrowth of a change in economic thinking in the 1970s. Since then, the economic promise of globalization has not materialized, according to Saul. Any small gains, Saul says, are actually just the result of the rich getting richer. Despite economic gains in the developing world, Saul argues that these gains are not the result of embracing globalization. Brookes is the editorial director of Progressive Book Club and former Web editor for *Mother Jones* magazine. Saul is a Canadian essayist and novelist and is the author of *The Collapse of Globalism and the Reinvention of the World.*

AS YOU READ, CONSIDER THE FOLLOWING QUESTIONS:

1. As cited by Brookes, what two political leaders took up the cause of globalization in the 1980s?

2. How does Saul characterize the economic growth of the last thirty years of globalization?
3. According to Saul, how does the West feel about the increasing exports coming out of China and India?

The current wave of globalization has its origins in the economic crises of the 1970s, when the industrialized economies, after three decades of steady growth, began to flounder, beset by persistently high unemployment and inflation, and governments began casting around for an alternative to the Keynesian orthodoxy [theory based on the ideas of economist John Maynard Keynes] that had dominated economic thinking since the end of the Second World War. They found that alternative in a (hitherto fringe) school of thought associated with Friedrich von Hayek and, later, Milton Friedman, one premised on the notion that in matters of economic management government was the problem, not part of the solution, as Keynesianism had it.

The Doctrine of Globalization
Central to the new thinking—taken up famously and with particular fervor in the 1980s by Margaret Thatcher and Ronald Reagan—was the idea that market forces work best and to everyone's benefit when government stands aside. Left alone, such forces would inevitably unleash waves of trade, which would in turn generate a tide of growth, raising all ships in both the developed and developing world. Deregulation and privatization were the watchwords of the day.

Developing countries were effectively forced to open up to foreign trade and capital—for their own good. On a global scale, the embrace of what fast became a new orthodoxy promised an impressive array of social and political benefits as trade barriers fell and international markets were freed from the dead hand of government: the power of the nation-state would wane; nationalism and racism would fade; economics, not politics—and certainly not religion—would shape human events. Free markets and free democracies would become the norm in an interdependent, peaceful world held together by the magic of enlightened self-interest.

The Collapse of Free Trade Orthodoxy

However, as John Ralston Saul argues in his new book, *The Collapse of Globalism*, things didn't work out quite as planned. The past three decades have been marked by unimpressive economic growth and sharply increasing economic inequality, and recent years have seen a marked rise in economic populism, nationalism, and conflict, much of it *within* states. The Asian financial crisis of 1997–98 pointed up the instability of the global economic system, and, in 1998, the talks

Economist John Ralston Saul (pictured with his wife) says that globalization has brought about the collapse of free trade principles, a problem that must be addressed by the nations of the world.

on the Multilateral Agreement on Investment (MAI) collapsed. In 1999, the WTO [World Trade Organization] conference at Seattle drew huge protests that derailed the talks. As the failure of last week's free trade meeting [Fourth Summit of the Americas, November 4–5, 2005] in Argentina showed, developing countries, having gradually and painfully discovered that globalization, at least as currently conceived by the industrialized countries, has been something less than a boon, are no longer willing to open their markets with no questions asked, on terms dictated by the United States and other industrialized countries.

Saul, a Canadian, writes that the collapse of free trade orthodoxy has left us in a vacuum, unmoored from the (spurious) certainties of yesterday's economic fundamentalism but lacking a better framework for thinking about economic arrangements within and among states.

FAST FACT

The world's largest multinational, or transnational, corporation in 2008 was Wal-Mart, with over $378 billion in revenue.

The task of figuring out what that framework might be requires, first of all, that the proponents of globalization admit that there's a problem with their model, which many have been unwilling to do.

Saul is the author of many books, including *Voltaire's Bastards*. He recently talked with *Mother Jones* by phone from Canada.

The Economic Effect of Globalization

Mother Jones: *It's fairly clear that some of the wilder political predictions of globalization theorists—the decline of nationalism, the fading away of sectarian passions, for example—have fallen short. But you argue that the economic promise hasn't panned out, either.*

John Ralston Saul: That's right. Look, we've seen a 22 times increase in world trade, a 15 times increase in foreign investment, incredible multiples in financial markets. Traditionally in capitalism, when you have more cash, you can fund more activity, which produces more jobs and creates more wealth. That's basic economic theory. But in fact you find that this 30-year period has been a time of average or below-average growth. Interestingly, the Keynesian period,

Beliefs About the Effects of Globalization in America

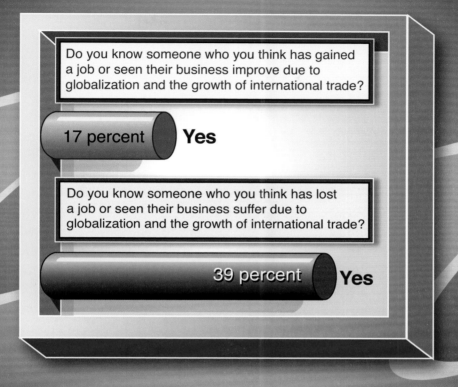

Do you know someone who you think has gained a job or seen their business improve due to globalization and the growth of international trade?

17 percent Yes

Do you know someone who you think has lost a job or seen their business suffer due to globalization and the growth of international trade?

39 percent Yes

Taken from: "Americans on Globalization, Trade, and Farm Subsidies," Program on International Policy Attitudes (PIPA) and Knowledge Networks, January 22, 2004.

covering the previous 25 years, was a period of *high taxes and high growth.* So you stand back and you say, "So, we got this growth in trade and investment and money markets, and we didn't get even an above-average growth. Why not? Why hasn't it worked? And why aren't we discussing the fact that it hasn't worked?"

What about economic equality among and within nations? Is that another sign that something's amiss?

Yes, and the statistics show this pretty much everywhere. And the interesting thing is, even that disparity between rich and poor doesn't total up to a big increase in wealth; it's just that a small group of people are getting richer and a much larger group of people are getting poorer. So getting more of the pie today, for the poor, still wouldn't represent a success for the system. This suggests that the system, as designed by the globalists, simply isn't delivering what it said it would deliver. . . .

The Developing World

OK, but haven't millions of people in, say, India and China, the 21st century's rising economic powers, benefited enormously from globalization?

What you're seeing with India and China is the building and rebuilding of nation states on their own model. The Chinese are really going back to the Middle Kingdom view of themselves, and in the case of India they have a history as a nation state very different from the European one. In a sense they're building something that's about the nation. Does this mean they don't want to trade with the world? No, of course not. But they're not buying into globalist theories of inevitability. They have some stuff to sell; they want to sell it.

What's interesting is how much difficulty we're having with them. We actually don't want to give them the kind of access to our markets that we expected would be a normal part of globalization. And I think what it tells you is that for 25 years we've said what matters is globalization; borders don't matter; nation states are weakening; it's the global market place that matters. And suddenly we're saying, "Hey, you can't export all that stuff to us, that's not fair." And so you suddenly realize that what we were always saying is that globalization is great—as long as it's based out of the West.

> **EVALUATING THE AUTHORS' ARGUMENTS:**
>
> In this viewpoint Saul claims that globalization has increased economic inequality both within and among nations. If this is true, does this concern at all diminish Tyler Cowen's claim in favor of globalization in the previous viewpoint—that the resulting innovation could be of benefit to everyone? Explain.

The Poor Are Benefiting from Globalization

John L. Manzella

"Trade and globalization have improved the lives of billions of people in developing countries."

In the following viewpoint John L. Manzella contends that globalization is causing a worldwide reduction in poverty. He argues that openness to trade distinguishes the fastest-growing developing countries from the slowest. Although Manzella admits that some developing countries are unable to participate in globalization, he insists that globalization will help alleviate economic ills, and that a better way must be found to harness globalization to help the world's poorest, most marginalized countries. John L. Manzella is a trade consultant and the author of the book *Grasping Globalization: Its Impact and Your Corporate Response.*

AS YOU READ, CONSIDER THE FOLLOWING QUESTIONS:

1. According to Manzella, the number of people living in extreme poverty in East Asia and the Pacific decreased between 1990 and 1998 by what percentage?
2. How many years does it take for open economies to double in size compared to closed economies, according to Manzella?
3. What are the potential gains if world merchandise trade barriers are eliminated?

John L. Manzella, "Have Trade and Globalization Harmed Developing Countries?" *World Trade,* vol. 19, no. 1, January 2006, p. 8. Copyright © 2006 Business News Publishing Co.

The answer to the question, "has globalization harmed developing countries?," is "No!" Quite the contrary, in fact. Trade and globalization have improved the lives of billions of people in developing countries. For example, in the short span of 1990 through 1998, the number of people living in extreme poverty in East Asia and the Pacific decreased 41 percent—one of the largest and most rapid reductions in history.

Advantages of Globalization

Today, 24 developing countries representing about 3 billion people, including China, India and Mexico, have adopted policies enabling their citizens to take advantage of globalization. The net result is that their economies are catching up with rich ones.

Over the last two decades, according to the World Bank, these 24 countries achieved higher growth in incomes, longer life expectancy and better schooling. The incomes of the least globalized countries during this same period, including Iran, Pakistan and North Korea, dropped or remained static. What distinguishes the fastest growing developing countries from the slowest is clear: their openness to trade.

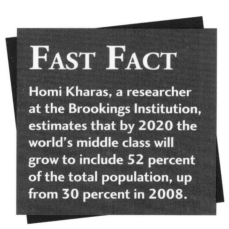

FAST FACT

Homi Kharas, a researcher at the Brookings Institution, estimates that by 2020 the world's middle class will grow to include 52 percent of the total population, up from 30 percent in 2008.

For many of the world's poorest countries, the primary problem is not too much globalization, but their inability to participate in it. Study after study corroborate this. For example, the WTO [World Trade Organization] report, *Trade, Income Disparity and Poverty,* says, "Trade liberalization helps poor countries catch up with rich ones," and concludes that trade liberalization "is essential if poor people are to have any hope of a brighter future."

Globalization, Poverty and Inequality, published by the Progressive Policy Institute, contends that less globalization is generally associated with less development, and concludes that no country has managed to lift itself out of poverty without integrating into the global economy.

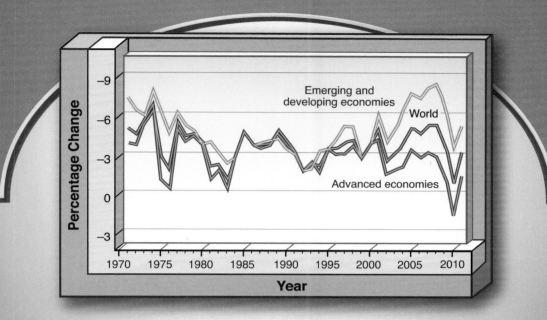

Gross Domestic Product (GDP)* Worldwide

*Gross domestic product (GDP) is the value of a country's overall output of goods and services within its borders during a specific period.

Taken from: Trendlines Research, www.trendlines.ca, February 17, 2009./International Monetary Fund (IMF).

And who would know this better than former Mexican President Ernesto Zedillo, who said, "In every case where a poor nation has significantly overcome its poverty, this has been achieved while engaging in production for export markets and opening itself to the influx of foreign goods, investment and technology—that is, by participating in globalization."

Globalization Alleviates Economic Ills

Even former sociologist Fernando Henrique Cardoso, who spoke out against aspects of global dependence, promoted—not resisted—globalization as president of Brazil.

Developing countries with open economies grew by 4.5 percent a year in the 1970s and 1980s, while those with closed economies grew

A Chinese couple checks the latest fashions at a market in Beijing. From 1990 to 2004, 407 million Chinese escaped poverty due to economic reforms and the benefits of globalization.

by 0.7 percent a year, concludes the National Bureau of Economic Research report, *Economic Convergence and Economic Policies.* At this rate, open economies double in size every 16 years, while closed economies double every 100 years.

Globalization may not be a panacea for all economic ills, but it certainly helps alleviate them. However, it has had negative consequences on some developing countries with distorted economies or a lack of sound legal or financial systems. As a result, anti-globalists with good intentions but bad policy recommendations often make globalization the scapegoat for many of the world's problems.

In the end, the facts don't lie. Since the 1970s—when policies supporting globalization got traction—through 2001, world infant mortality rates decreased by almost half, adult literacy increased more than a third, primary school enrollment rose and the average life span shot up 11 years. Looking forward, from 2002 through 2025, life expectancy is projected to rise from 62 years to 68 years in less developed countries, the U.S. Census Bureau estimates.

Removing World Trade Barriers
Will Help Developing Countries

The World Bank report, Globalization, Growth and Poverty: Building an Inclusive World Economy, suggests that globalization must be better harnessed to help the world's poorest, most marginalized countries improve the lives of their citizens—an especially important effort in the wake of [the] September 11 [2001 terrorist attacks on the World Trade Center]. Agreed. But how to achieve this is not yet known.

In the meantime consider this. If remaining world merchandise trade barriers are eliminated, potential gains are estimated at $250 to $650 billion annually, according to the International Monetary Fund and World Bank. About one-third to one-half of these gains would accrue in developing countries. Removal of agricultural supports would raise global economic welfare by an additional $128 billion annually, with some $30 billion going to developing countries.

EVALUATING THE AUTHOR'S ARGUMENTS:

In this viewpoint Manzella argues that globalization is lifting numerous people out of poverty around the globe. Does his background as a trade consultant add to or detract from his argument in your opinion?

The Poor Are Getting Poorer from Globalization

"Relative inequalities are exploding, and the world's poorest, despite all the advantages of globalisation, may even be getting poorer."

Noreena Hertz

In the following viewpoint Noreena Hertz argues that globalization is not benefiting the poor. She contends that much of the research done on economic globalization is confined to aggregate economic data, so the figures of the gross domestic product, or GDP, tell us nothing about who gains and who loses. Hertz claims that if we allow trade interests to continue to dominate, we shall never reconnect the social with the economic. Hertz is the author of *The Silent Takeover*.

AS YOU READ, CONSIDER THE FOLLOWING QUESTIONS:

1. What does the author mean by "exclusion?"
2. Why does the author claim that a World Social Organization must be created?
3. What are some of the mechanisms the author suggests to help people fight against injustice?

Noreena Hertz, "EXCLUSION," *New Statesman*, vol. 130, no. 4560, October 22, 2001, pp. 22(4).

We live increasingly in a world of haves and have-nots, of gated communities next to ghettos, of extreme poverty and unbelievable riches. Some enjoy rights that are completely denied to others. Relative inequalities are exploding, and the world's poorest, despite all the advances of globalisation, may even be getting poorer.

The World's Poorest Are Getting Poorer

It is a world of extremes, which can be characterised most clearly in terms of exclusion. That means political exclusion, whereby the rights of citizens are marginalised by the interests of big business: George W Bush's environmental policy, for example, is clearly formulated in the interests of US energy companies. It means economic exclusion: in almost every developing country, the numbers living on less than a dollar a day have increased in the past 20 years. And it means social exclusion, which prevents billions from gaining redress for injustices: Brazilian tobacco workers, for example, are poisoned by outlawed pesticides, but they have no hope of compensation, let alone an improvement in their working conditions.

These issues must be addressed, not only for the sake of the two million and more children each year who die of diarrhoea for lack

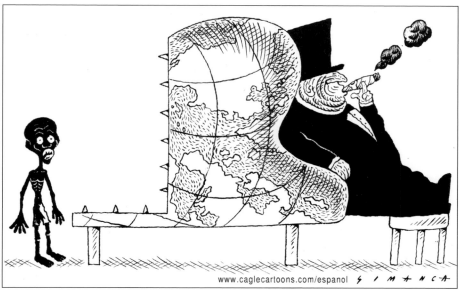

"Globalization," cartoon by Simanca Osmani, Cagle Cartoons, Brazil. Copyright © 2007 by Best of Latin America and CagleCartoons.com. All rights reserved.

of clean water, but for our own sakes. If they are not addressed, a growing movement of people will make even our gated communities impossible to protect.

We must embrace a new agenda based on inclusiveness; a commitment to reconnecting the social and the economic; a relinking of the latter to a plausible redistributive system; and a determination to ensure that everyone has access to justice. All these things are within our reach.

The Impact of Economic Globalisation Must Be Investigated

First, an international independent commission should investigate the impact of economic globalisation. This should be transparent and open. It should involve representatives of the south as well as the north, the poor as well as the rich. It should ask: what is the impact of trade liberalisation on the global poor? What is the cost of economic growth to the environment? What price do we pay for allowing big business to influence the rules on the quality of our air and food? How do we justify allowing the north to protect industries such as agriculture and textiles while the south is told to open up all its markets? What are the implications for society when rural communities collapse overnight; or for farmers when corporations patent indigenous plants?

FAST FACT

According to World Bank *World Development Indicators* in 2008, the poorest one-fifth of the world consumes 1.5 percent of the world's goods, whereas the richest one-fifth consumes 76.6 percent.

We do not know the answers to all these questions. Much of the research is confined to aggregate economic data; figures of rising GDP [gross domestic product] tell us nothing about who gains and who loses. And there is no public forum in which these issues can be rigorously examined. Now, more than ever, we need to confront the beliefs of the market fundamentalists away from the streets. Second, we must create a World Social Organisation, to reframe market mechanisms in rules and regulations

Children in this Honduran shanty school will benefit from the International Monetary Fund's Poverty Reduction and Growth Facility program by getting a new school built. Nonetheless, despite the IMF's efforts, poverty continues to rise worldwide.

that ensure that the costs of, for example, pollution and human rights abuses are factored in to all economic activity. This organisation needs teeth as sharp as those of the WTO [World Trade Organization], and equally effective powers of enforcement.

If we allow trade interests to continue to dominate, we shall never reconnect the social with the economic. We shall perpetuate a system that too often puts the interests of big business before people, and profit before social or environmental justice. But we must be careful that the north does not use this new organisation as a form of protectionism. The developed world should help developing countries with the costs of better global regulation; and, in the short term at least, the south should meet different requirements.

There still remains the problem of alleviating the positions of those who are most excluded and marginalised. At the least, this means the cancellation of debt, reversing the outflows of capital from the south to the north. Overseas aid, which to the least developed countries has fallen 45 per cent in real terms since 1990, must be significantly increased, while the ways in which it is delivered must be rethought.

But we also need new resources to give people access to better lives. These can be raised only by a global tax authority, which would raise global indirect taxes—on the use of energy and resources and on pollution—and then redistribute them.

Dealing with Exclusion

Finally, we need mechanisms to help people fight against injustice. All people, wherever they are, must be extended the rights we take for granted: minimum health and safety standards, minimum wages, protection from being dispossessed without adequate compensation.

In the long term, this involves strengthening the local and international regulation of companies and making enforcement effective. But governments of countries in which multinationals are domiciled can take steps now. In several test cases, companies are being sued in the north for actions carried out by their subsidiaries in the south. They include Unocal, being sued in the US in connection with its activities in Burma; and Cape, being sued in the UK [United Kingdom] in connection with its activities in South Africa. But this means of redress is usually blocked on two fronts. First, it is very seldom possible to lift the corporate veil and make parent companies accountable for the actions of their subsidiaries. Second, even when this is done, there are usually no funds available for workers or communities to take on wealthy multinationals.

So, to ensure that the perpetrators of corporate crimes can be held to account, wherever they are, and to ensure that their victims have redress, whoever they are, we need two things. First, we need legislation so that parent companies can be held responsible for the actions of their subsidiaries. Second, we need a global legal aid fund so that workers and communities everywhere get access to justice.

A tall order? Perhaps; but after 11 September [2001], it is clearer than ever that our divided world cannot continue as it is. Terrorism and trade cannot be the only issues on which the world unites. We must commit ourselves to a global coalition to deal with exclusion, too.

EVALUATING THE AUTHORS' ARGUMENTS:

In this viewpoint, Hertz disagrees with John L. Manzella's claim in the previous viewpoint that the poor are benefiting from globalization. At the conclusion of both articles, the authors mention September 11—why do you think it was important for both authors to mention this?

Globalization Increases Ethical Outcomes and Improves Moral Character

Jagdish N. Bhagwati

"Globalization . . . leads not only to the creation and spread of wealth but to ethical outcomes and to better moral character among its participants."

In the following viewpoint Jagdish N. Bhagwati argues that globalization leads to a more ethical world. Bhagwati responds to the concerns of some critics who say that globalization makes things worse for the progress of ethical agendas such as gender equity; to the contrary, Bhagwati claims that globalization actually increases these ethical outcomes. Additionally, he believes that globalization has a positive effect on moral character worldwide. Bhagwati is professor of economics and law at Columbia University, senior fellow for international economics at the Council on Foreign Relations, and the author of *In Defense of Globalization.*

AS YOU READ, CONSIDER THE FOLLOWING QUESTIONS:
  1. What example does Bhagwati give to support his claim that globalization is good for children of poor peasants?
  2. According to the author, critics of globalization make the implausible claim that globalization makes people selfish and vicious because of what?
  3. What example from the 1980s does Bhagwati give to show how the increased global movement caused by globalization leads to positive social reform?

I can attest from personal experience that, if you try to talk about the free market on today's university campuses, you will be buried in an avalanche of criticism of globalization. The opposition of faculty and students to the expansion of international markets stems largely from a sense of altruism. It proceeds from their concern about social and moral issues. Simply put, they believe that globalization lacks a human face. I take an opposite view. Globalization, I would argue, leads not only to the creation and spread of wealth but to ethical outcomes and to better moral character among its participants.

The Ethical Outcomes of Globalization

Many critics believe that globalization sets back social and ethical agendas, such as the reduction of child labor and poverty in poor countries and the promotion of gender equality and environmental protection everywhere. Yet, when I examined these and other issues in my book, *In Defense of Globalization*, I found that the actual outcomes were the opposite of those feared.

For example, many believed that poor peasants would respond to the greater economic opportunities presented by globalization by taking their children out of school and putting them to work. Thus considered, the extension of the free market would act as a malign force. But I found that the opposite was true. It turned out that in many instances, the higher incomes realized as a result of globalization—the rising earnings of rice growers in Vietnam, for example—spurred parents to keep their children in school. After all, they no longer needed the meager income that an additional child's labor could provide.

Jagdish N. Bhagwati, professor of economics at Columbia University and the viewpoint's author, writes that globalization has had a positive effect on ethical standards and moral character around the world.

Or consider gender equality. With globalization, industries that produce traded goods and services face intensified international competition. This competition has reduced the yawning gap in many developing countries between the compensation paid to equally qualified male and female workers. Why? Because firms competing globally soon find that they cannot afford to indulge their pro-male prejudices. Under pressure to reduce costs and operate more efficiently, they shift increasingly from more expensive male labor to cheaper female labor, thus increasing female wages and reducing male wages. Globalization hasn't produced wage equality yet, but it has certainly narrowed the gap.

There is now plenty of evidence that India and China, two countries with gigantic poverty problems, have been able to grow so fast by taking advantage of trade and foreign investment, and that by doing so, they have reduced poverty dramatically. They still have a long way to go, but globalization has allowed them to improve material conditions for hundreds of millions of their people. Some critics have denounced the idea of attacking poverty through economic growth as a conservative "trickle-down" strategy. They evoke images of overfed, gluttonous nobles and bourgeoisie eating legs of mutton while the serfs and dogs under the table feed on scraps and crumbs. In truth, focusing on growth is better described as an activist "pull-up" strategy. Growing economies pull the poor up into gainful employment and reduce poverty.

The Concern About Moral Character

Even if they grant that globalization generally helps the achievement of certain social aims, some critics still argue that it corrodes moral character. A widening free market, they say, expands the domain over which profits are pursued, and profit-seeking makes people selfish and vicious. But this is hardly plausible.

Consider the Calvinist burghers described by Simon Schama in his history of the Netherlands. They made their fortunes from international trade, but they indulged their altruism rather than their personal appetites, exhibiting what Schama aptly called the "embarrassment of riches." Similar self-restraint can be seen in the Jains of Gujerat [Jainism is one of the oldest religions originating in India], the Indian state that Mahatma Gandhi came from. The riches that the Jains reaped from their commercial activities were harnessed to their values, not the other way around.

FAST FACT

According to a 2006 report by the World Economic Forum, the world has on average closed over 90 percent of the gender gap in education and in health.

A Shrinking World

As for the influence that globalization continues to have on moral character, let me quote the wonderful sentiments of [British philosopher and economist] John Stuart Mill. As he wrote in *Principles of Political Economy* (1848):

> The economical advantages of commerce are surpassed in importance by those of its effects, which are intellectual and moral. It is hardly possible to overrate the value, in the present low state of human improvement, of placing human beings in contact with persons dissimilar to themselves, and with modes of thought and action unlike those with which they are familiar. . . . There is no nation which does not need to borrow from others, not merely particular arts or practices, but essential points of character in which its own type is inferior. . . . It may be said without exag-

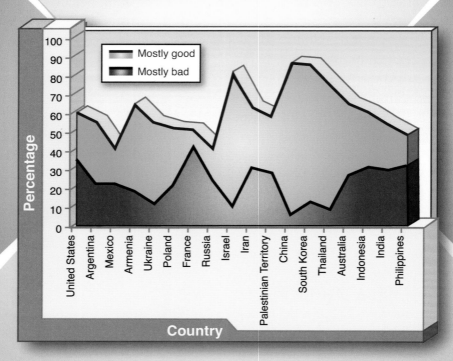

Globalization: Good or Bad?

In a 2007 poll, people in various countries were asked whether they felt that globalization was mostly good or mostly bad.

Mostly good
Mostly bad

Percentage

Country

United States, Argentina, Mexico, Armenia, Ukraine, Poland, France, Russia, Israel, Iran, Palestinian Territory, China, South Korea, Thailand, Australia, Indonesia, India, Philippines

Taken from: WorldPublicOpinion.org, 2007. www.worldpublicopinion.org/pipa/articles/btglobalizationtradera/349.php?lb=btgl&pnt=349&nid=&id=.

geration that the great extent and rapid increase in international trade, in being the principal guarantee of the peace of the world, is the great permanent security for the uninterrupted progress of the ideas, the institutions, and the character of the human race.

In today's global economy, we continually see signs of the phenomena Mill described. When Japanese multinationals spread out in the 1980s, their male executives brought their wives with them to New York, London, and Paris. When these traditional Japanese women saw how women were treated in the West, they absorbed ideas about women's rights and equality. When they returned to Japan, they became agents of social reform. In our own day, television and the Internet have played a huge role in expanding our social and moral consciousness beyond the bounds of our communities and nation-states.

[Eighteenth century economist] Adam Smith famously wrote of "a man of humanity in Europe" who would not "sleep tonight" if "he was to lose his little finger tomorrow" but would "snore with the most profound security" if a hundred million of his Chinese brethren were "suddenly swallowed up by an earthquake," because "he had never seen them." For us, the Chinese are no longer invisible, living at the outside edge of what [Scottish philosopher] David Hume called the concentric circles of our empathy. Last summer's [2008] earthquake in China, whose tragic aftermath was instantly transmitted onto our screens, was met by the rest of the world not with indifference but with empathy and a profound sense of moral obligation to the Chinese victims. It was globalization's finest hour.

EVALUATING THE AUTHOR'S ARGUMENTS:

In this viewpoint Bhagwati gives examples of how globalization has allowed ideas and information to be transmitted easily around the globe, resulting in improved moral character. What example might a critic of globalization give in support of the view that this open movement of ideas and information can also have negative effects?

Globalization Allows Corrupt Countries to Become More Corrupt

Branko Milanovic

"Intensified trade and travel have enabled the rise of corrupt states that thrive on illegal businesses."

In the following viewpoint Branko Milanovic contends that globalization has the effect of allowing corrupt nations to thrive and grow: Because globalization allows greater access to all kinds of markets worldwide, illegal markets have expanded alongside legal ones. Furthermore, Milanovic believes that governance alone will not solve the corruption problem. Milanovic is a lead economist in the World Bank's research department, where he works on the topics of income inequality and globalization, and is an associate scholar with the Carnegie Endowment for International Peace. He is the author of *Worlds Apart: Measuring International and Global Inequality* and *Income and Influence: Social Policy in Emerging Economies*.

AS YOU READ, CONSIDER THE FOLLOWING QUESTIONS:
  1. What examples does the author give of illegal goods and services that have provided soaring profits for corrupt states in the age of globalization?
  2. What percent of overall trade does the narcotics trade constitute, according to a report cited by Milanovic?
  3. What does the author think should be done about activities such as prostitution and drug use, in an effort to eliminate corruption?

It's become a cliché that globalization in the sense of greater integration of the world economies has brought both pain and gain. But in the general painting of the dark side of globalization, one aspect is frequently ignored: Intensified trade and travel have enabled the rise of corrupt states that thrive on illegal businesses. Only by changing the rules of the same global trade that has allowed corrupt states to grow can one hope to remove this blot on globalization.

Corrupt States

"Corrupt states" are different from a more commonly used category of "failed states." The distinguishing characteristic of a failed state is its inability to exercise control over its national territory; a key feature of a corrupt state is its weak governance structure, lawlessness and inability to move toward self-sustained development. While failed states have existed in the past—think of the Ottoman Empire in its last century—the spread of corrupt or criminalized states is a recent phenomenon, almost non-existent before the current wave of globalization. Is this a coincidence?

Globalization influences the relative profitability of different activities. In the US, globalization reduced profitability of steel production and increased it for software. In corrupt states, profitability soars in the production of goods and services that are internationally illegal: drugs, sex trafficking, contraband weapons or cigarettes, or counterfeit goods.

The best examples of corrupt states are found in the less developed parts of Europe, Asia and Latin America, exemplified by Albania, a regional center for human trafficking and cigarette and

Farmers work a poppy field in Afghanistan. In corrupt states profitability soars when the production of most goods is meant for illegal trafficking.

drug smuggling; Burma and Afghanistan, key drug-producing countries; and Paraguay, center of arms smuggling and counterfeit goods, and Colombia, the largest coca producer in the world. And indeed, in both 2005 and 2006, according to two World Bank governance indicators—control of corruption and rule of law—Albania is the most corrupt and lawless European country, exclusive of several former USSR [Union of Soviet Socialist Republics] countries, followed by Kosovo, the UN [United Nations]–administered territory that shares many characteristics. In Asia, Burma and Afghanistan easily top the list, again in both aspects of misgovernance. In Latin America, Haiti and Paraguay are deemed the most corrupt with Colombia somewhat better ranked, but still significantly below the continent's average.

Globalization's Role in Corruption

Globalization's contributed by creating new suppliers—for example, Albania could not supply people and guns while it was a closed state. More significantly, globalization reduced transportation costs, bringing these goods and services within the reach of the middle classes in the rich world. East European women are shipped to Western Europe because they are willing to provide sex services more cheaply than the local prostitutes, while their illegal status keeps them firmly in the grip of the mafias.

Low transportation costs help Moroccans and Nigerian "illegals" come to Spain, or Albanians and Moldovans go to Italy and France.

While, according to the 2007 UN report, the overall production and use of narcotics have stabilized (about 5 percent of adult world population is estimated to be annual users of opiates), the unit street-price is down and the global value of the narcotics trade is staggering. It is estimated at 5 to 6 percent of overall world trade, slightly larger than the combined global trade in agricultural products and cars. As in the case of electronics, toys, textiles or mineral water, the costs of producing and transporting drugs, women, weapons or copy-cat products have declined—and globalization opened up new possibilities for countries to specialize.

Governance Will Not Work

But, from an economist's perspective and leaving ethical issues aside, why would specialization in drugs, sex or guns be any different from specialization in textiles or computer chips? The reason lies in the illegality of the transactions, which naturally attracts entrepreneurs who, in addition to the usual business acumen, possess a requisite dose of ruthlessness. Enter the so-called "mafiya."

Once organized crime and its supporters become the largest employers in the country, they play the same role that a more conventional business plays in

> **FAST FACT**
>
> In 2008 the International Trade Union Confederation (ITUC) reported that data worldwide showed that women are paid 16 percent less than their male counterparts, on average.

other countries. They try to influence the political process. Moreover, they need to control the political arena—election of presidents and parliaments—even more tightly than "normal" business people because their very existence depends on having a government willing to tolerate violation of international rules as the country's main activity.

The government structure that emerges is "endogenous": It reflects domestic social and economic structure, which in turn is the outcome of greater international trade and economic incentives, much like other countries, except that the governance structure is, almost inevitably, more corrupt. The recent World Bank and International Monetary Fund's insistence on reforming governance in these countries is bound to fail because the cause is misdiagnosed.

Governance is viewed by the international organizations as something "exogenous," something that a country just happens to have and

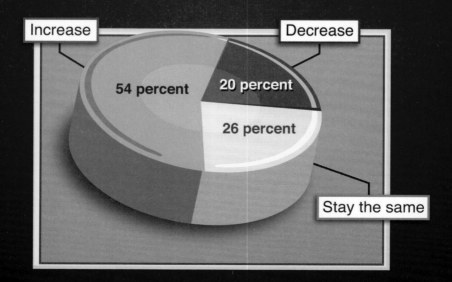

Perception of Worldwide Corruption

When polled about corruption levels, a majority of people around the world think that corruption will increase.

Percentage of respondents reporting that in three years corruption will:

Increase

54 percent

Decrease

20 percent

26 percent

Stay the same

which—through a better electoral process, more transparent laws and more honest lawmakers—can be improved. Thus the international organizations are in a permanent, and fruitless, search of an "honest" lawmaker, an Eliot Ness [framed Mafia fighter during Prohibition] who will bust corruption and illegality. They fail to notice that governance structures respond to underlying incentives, and to expect an honest person to rise to power in a corrupt state is akin to expecting a person with no financial backing from big business to be elected president of the US. In both cases, the outcome of a political process reflects the country's underlying economic conditions.

The Legalization Solution

A different approach is necessary: legalize the currently illegal activities like prostitution and drug use and modify the often draconian US and European immigration laws that stimulate human trafficking. If prostitution and drugs indeed became like haircuts and candies, their production would obey the same rules: Countries that export beauty services and confectionary products are not notably more corrupt than others. Some of the current entrepreneurs would remain in these activities, others would move to others. In either case, there would be a general "normalization" akin to what was observed after prohibition on alcohol sales was lifted in the US. Thousands of "bootleggers" became normal producers of alcohol, alcohol-linked criminality decreased, and only a minority of those with preference for high risk and crime moved to other illegal activities.

Most people involved in illegal activities today are not doing it because they love crime and are intrinsically different from the so-called law-abiding citizens. They do it because the gains are so high. Or to give another example: They're no different from "normal" businessmen in Eastern Europe, Asia and Latin America who violate the law rather than pay exorbitant taxes but would, if taxes were reduced, rush to become "legal."

The key is that meaningful reforms do not begin in the corrupt states themselves, but in the rich world that is the main consumer of illegal goods and services. This requires a total overhaul in our thinking about the root cause of a corrupt state. Many of the most corrupt states are "corrupt" because they specialize in goods and services that are deemed illegal. But what is illegal today is not necessarily illegal tomorrow. "Illegality" is a historical category, as the long history of accepted prostitution and drug use shows. Thus if illegality is the main cause of corrupt governments, then the best way to root out corruption is to remove illegality.

The way to help corrupt countries does not lie in hectoring them about the virtue of good governance, but in pushing for the legalization of their main exports. The target constituency of the international organizations' advocacy thus becomes the rich, not the poor, world.

EVALUATING THE AUTHORS' ARGUMENTS:

Milanovic's claim that globalization allows corrupt nations to become more corrupt contradicts Jagdish N. Bhagwati's claim in the previous viewpoint that globalization improves moral character. Do you think Bhagwati would agree with Milanovic's proposed solution to corruption? Why or why not?

Chapter 3

What Are Some Concerns About Globalization?

International shipping containers await processing at the Port of Oakland in California.

Globalization Has Not Reached Its Potential

"Unless we recognize and address the problems of globalization, it will be difficult to sustain."

Joseph E. Stiglitz

In the following viewpoint Joseph E. Stiglitz contends that globalization has the potential to make life better for everyone. However, he argues that problems need to be addressed in order for globalization to continue. He suggests that some domestic changes could help counteract the negative effects of globalization, and he stresses the need for effective international organizations. Stiglitz is a professor of economics at the Graduate School of Arts and Sciences, Business School, and School of International and Public Affairs at Columbia University. He is the author of *Making Globalization Work.*

AS YOU READ, CONSIDER THE FOLLOWING QUESTIONS:

1. Is the author a member of the antiglobalization movement?
2. According to Stiglitz, what has happened to the real wages of low-wage workers for the past three decades?
3. What three institutions, according to the author, are needed now more than ever?

I have written repeatedly about the problems of globalization: an unfair global trade regime that impedes development; an unstable global financial system that results in recurrent crises, with poor countries repeatedly finding themselves burdened with unsustainable debt; and a global intellectual property regime that denies access to affordable life-saving drugs, even as AIDS ravages the developing world.

The Problems of Globalization

I have also written about globalization's anomalies: money should flow from rich to poor countries, but in recent years it has been going in the opposite direction. While the rich are better able to bear the risks of currency and interest-rate fluctuations, it is the poor who bear the brunt of this volatility.

Indeed, I have complained so loudly and vociferously about the problems of globalization that many have wrongly concluded that I belong to the anti-globalization movement. But I believe that globalization has enormous potential—as long as it is properly managed.

Some 70 years ago, during the Great Depression, [British economist] John Maynard Keynes formulated his theory of unemployment, which described how government action could help restore full employment. While conservatives vilified him, Keynes actually did more to save the capitalist system than all the pro-market financiers put together. Had the conservatives been followed, the Great Depression would have been even worse and the demand for an alternative to capitalism would have grown stronger.

By the same token, unless we recognize and address the problems of globalization, it will be difficult to sustain. Globalization is not inevitable: there have been setbacks before, and there can be setbacks again.

The Potential for Globalization

Globalization's advocates are right that it has the *potential* to raise everyone's living standards. But it has not done that. The questions posed by young French workers, who wonder how globalization will make them better off if it means accepting lower wages and weaker job protection, can no longer be ignored. Nor can such questions be

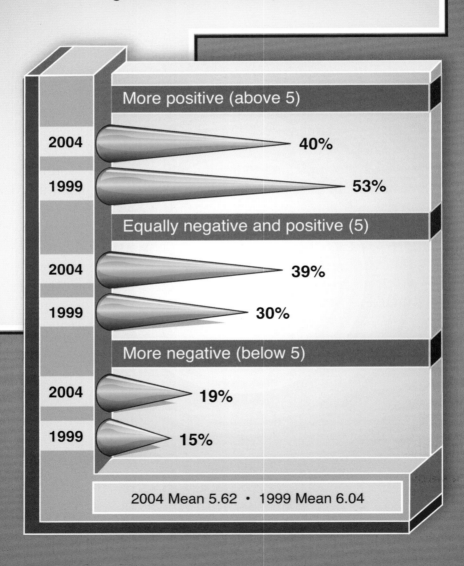

Views on Globalization

How positive or negative is the process of globalization overall (1–10)?

More positive (above 5)

2004 — 40%

1999 — 53%

Equally negative and positive (5)

2004 — 39%

1999 — 30%

More negative (below 5)

2004 — 19%

1999 — 15%

2004 Mean 5.62 • 1999 Mean 6.04

Taken from: "Americans on Globalization, Trade, and Farm Subsidies," Program on International Policy Attitudes (PIPA) and Knowledge Networks, January 22, 2004.

answered with the wistful hope that everyone will someday benefit. As Keynes pointed out, in the long run, we are all dead.

Growing inequality in the advanced industrial countries was a long-predicted but seldom advertised consequence of globalization. Full economic integration implies the equalization of unskilled wages everywhere in the world, and, though we are nowhere near attaining this "goal," the downward pressure on those at the bottom is evident.

To the extent that changes in technology have contributed to the near stagnation of real wages for low-skilled workers in the United States and elsewhere for the past three decades, there is little that citizens can do. But they *can* do something about globalization.

Economic theory does not say that everyone will win from glo-

balization, but only that the net gains will be positive, and that the winners can therefore compensate the losers and still come out ahead. But conservatives have argued that in order to remain competitive in a global world, taxes must be cut and the welfare state reduced. This has been done in the US, where taxes have become less progressive, with tax cuts given to the winners—those who benefit from both globalization and technological changes. As a result, the US and others following its example are becoming rich countries with poor people.

But the Scandinavian countries have shown that there is another way. Of course, government, like the private sector, must strive for efficiency. But investments in education and research, together with a strong social safety net, can lead to a more productive and competitive economy, with more security and higher living standards for all. A strong safety net and an economy close to full employment provides a conducive environment for all stakeholders—workers, investors, and entrepreneurs—to engage in the risk-taking that new investments and firms require.

The Need for Institutions

The problem is that economic globalization has outpaced the globalization of politics and mindsets. We have become more interdependent, increasing the need to act together, but we do not have the institutional frameworks for doing this effectively and democratically.

Never has the need for international organizations like the IMF [International Monetary Fund], the World Bank, and the World Trade Organization [WTO] been greater, and seldom has confidence in these institutions been lower. The world's lone superpower, the US, has demonstrated its disdain for supranational institutions and worked assiduously to undermine them. The looming failure of the Development Round of trade talks and the long delay in the United Nations Security Council's demand for a ceasefire in Lebanon are but the latest examples of America's contempt for multilateral initiatives.

Enhancing our understanding of globalization's problems will help us to formulate remedies—some small, some large—aimed at both providing symptomatic relief and addressing the underlying causes.

Joseph E. Stiglitz, 2001 Nobel Prize in Economics recipient, believes domestic changes in policy can counteract the negative effects of globalization through effective international organizations.

There is a broad array of policies that can benefit people in both developing and developed countries, thereby providing globalization with the popular legitimacy that it currently lacks.

In other words, globalization can be changed; indeed, it is clear that it *will* be changed. The question is whether change will be forced upon us by a crisis or result from careful, democratic deliberation and debate. Crisis-driven change risks producing a backlash against globalization, or a haphazard reshaping of it, thus merely setting the stage for more problems later on. By contrast, taking control of the process holds out the possibility of remaking globalization, so that it at last lives up to its potential and its promise: higher living standards for everyone in the world.

EVALUATING THE AUTHORS' ARGUMENTS:

Stiglitz cites investments in education and research and the strong social safety net in Scandinavian countries as potential ways to address the problems of globalization. Do you think Vandana Shiva, author of the next viewpoint, would be more in favor of globalization if individual countries made these changes? Why or why not?

Globalization Has a Polarizing Effect

Vandana Shiva

"The project of corporate Globalisation is a project for polarising and dividing people."

In the following viewpoint Vandana Shiva argues that globalization has divided people. She argues against the theory of the world as "flat," arguing that the globalization process has not been driven by individuals but has, instead, been driven by undemocratic institutions and corporations. Shiva is founder of the Research Foundation for Science, Technology, and Ecology, where she started the program Navdanya, a research initiative to provide direction and support to environmental activism, especially as it supports indigenous knowledge and culture. Shiva is the author of *Earth Democracy: Justice, Sustainability and Peace.*

AS YOU READ, CONSIDER THE FOLLOWING QUESTIONS:
1. What is the one way in which Shiva believes that Thomas L. Friedman's claim that the world is "flat" is accurate?
2. Shiva argues that e-commerce and the "walmartisation" of the economy was able to take place because of what?
3. How many people in India are employed in the information technology/outsourcing sector, according to the author?

Vandana Shiva, "The Polarised World of Globalisation," Zcommunications.org, May 28, 2005. Reproduced by permission.

T he project of corporate Globalisation is a project for polarising and dividing people—along axis of class and economic inequality, axis of religion and culture, axis of gender, axis of geographies and regions. Never before in human history has the gap between those who labour and those who accumulate wealth without labour been greater. Never before has hate between cultures been so global. Never before has there been a global convergence of three violent trends—the violence of primitive accumulation for wealth creation, the violence of "culture wars", and the violence of militarized warfare.

The Flat World Theory

Yet [columnist] Thomas [L.] Friedman describes this deeply divided world created by Globalisation and its multiple offsprings of insecurity and polarization as a "flat" world. In his book *The World Is Flat* Friedman tries desperately to argue that Globalisation is a leveller of inequalities in societies. But when you only look at the worldwide Web of information technology, and refuse to look at the web of life, the food web, the web of community, the web of local economies and local cultures which Globalisation is destroying, it is easy to make false and fallacious arguments that the world is flat.

When you look at the world perched on heights of arrogant, blind power, separated and disconnected from those who have lost their livelihoods, lifestyles, and lives—farmers and workers everywhere—it is easy to be blind both to the valleys of poverty and the mountains of affluence. Flat vision is a disease. But Friedman would like us to see his diseased, perverse flat view of globalisation's polarisations as a revolution that aims to reverse the revolutions that allowed us to see that the world is round and the earth goes round the sun, not the other way around.

Friedman has reduced the world to the friends he visits, the CEOs [chief executive officers] he knows, and the golf courses he plays at. From this microcosm of privilege, exclusion, blindness, he shuts out both the beauty of diversity and the brutality of exploitation and inequality, he shuts out the social and ecological externalities of economic globalisation and free trade, he shuts out the walls that globalisation is building—walls of insecurity and hatred and fear—walls of "intellectual property", walls of privatization.

In this viewpoint author Vandana Shiva, Indian physicist and environmental activist, disagrees with the views set forth by Thomas Friedman in his book The World Is Flat.

He focuses only on laws, regulations and policies which were the protections of the weak and the vulnerable, on barriers necessary as boundary conditions for the exercise of freedom and democracy, rights and justice, peace and security, sustainability and sharing of the earth's precious and vital resources. And he sees the dismantling of these ecological and social protections for deregulated commerce as a "flattening".

But this flattening is like the flattening of cities with bombs, the flattening of Asia's coasts by the tsunami, the flattening of forests and tribal homelands to build dams and mine minerals. Friedman's conceptualization of the world as flat is accurate only as a description of the social and ecological destruction caused by deregulated commerce or "free-trade". On every other count it is inaccurate and false.

The Real History of Globalisation

Take Friedman's description of the waves of globalisation. According to him, globalization 1.0 which lasted from 1492 when Columbus set sail to 1800 and shrank the world from a size large to a size medium, with countries and governments breaking down walls and knitting the world together. Globalisation 2.0 which lasted from 1800 to 2000, which shrank the world from a size medium to a size small, and the key agent of change was multinational companies. Globalisation 3.0 started in 2000, is shrinking the size small to size tiny, and it is being driven by individuals.

This is a totally false view of history. From one perspective in the south, the three waves of globalization have been based on the use of force, they have been driven by greed, and they have resulted in dispossession and displacement. For Native Americans, globalisation 1.0 started from 1492 and has still not ended.

For us in India the first wave of globalisation was driven by the first global corporation, the East India Company, working closely with the British team, and did not end till 1947 when we got Independence. We view the current phase as a recolonisation, with a similar partnership between multinational corporations and powerful governments. It is corporate led, not people led. And the current phase did not begin in 2000 as Friedman would have us believe. It began in the 1980s with the structural adjustment programmes of World Bank and IMF [International Monetary Fund] imposing trade liberalisation and privatization, and was accelerated since 1995 with the establishment of World Trade Organisation [WTO] at the end of the Uruguay Round of the General Agreement of Trade and Tariffs.

Friedman's false flat earth history then enables him to take two big leaps—results of coercive, undemocratic "free trade" treaties are reduced to achievements of information technology and corporate globalization and corporate control is presented as the collaborations and competition between individuals. The WTO, World Bank and IMF disappear, and the multinational corporations disappear. Globalisation is then about technological inevitability and individual innovativeness, not a project of powerful corporations aided by powerful institutions and powerful governments.

Undemocratic Corporate Control

Neither e-commerce nor walmartisation of the economy could take place without the dismantling of trade protections, workers protections, environmental protections. Technology of communication does not make long distance supply of goods, including food products, cheaper than local supply. Low wages, subsidies, externalisation of costs make Wal-Mart cheap, not its information technology–based supply chain management.

In 1988, I was in Berlin before the Berlin wall fell. We were part of the biggest ever mobilisation against the World Bank. Addressing a rally of nearly 100,000 people at the Berlin wall I had said that the Berlin wall should be dismantled as should the wall between rich and poor the World Bank creates by locking the Third World into debt, privatising our resources, and transforming our economies into markets for multinational corporations. I spoke about how the alliance between the World Bank and global corporations was establishing a centrally controlled, authoritarian rule like communism in its control, but different in the objective of profits as the only end of power. As movements we sought and fought for bringing down all walls of power and inequality.

Friedman's flat vision makes him blind to the emergence of corporate rule through the rules of corporate globalisation as the establishment of authoritarian rule and centrally controlled economies. He presents the collapse of the Berlin wall as having "tipped the balance of power across the world toward those advocating democratic, consensual, free-market-oriented governance, and away from those advocating authoritarian rule with centrally planned economies."

Movements Against Globalisation

Citizens' movements fighting globalisation advocate democratic, consensual governance and fight the WTO, the World Bank and global corporations precisely because they are undemocratic and dictatorial; they are authoritarian and centralized. The WTO agreement on Agriculture was drafted by [Dan] Amstutz, a Cargill [international food producer] official, who led the U.S negotiations on agriculture during the Uruguay Round and is now in-charge of Food and Agriculture in the Iraqi Constitution. This is a centrally planned authoritarian rule over food and farming.

That is why the democratic and consensual response of citizens' movements and Third World governments in Cancun led to the collapse of the WTO Ministerial. And it was the so called "flatteners" who were erecting walls—the barricades at which the Korean farmer Lee took his life, the walls that the U.S. Trade Representative Robert Zoellick tried to create between "Can do" and "Can't do" countries. What Zoellick and Friedman fail to see is that what they call "Can't do" is the "Can do" for the defense of farmers in the face of dumping and unfair trade. Their world is shaped by and focussed in Cargill—our world is shaped by and focussed on 300 million species and 6 billion people.

The biggest wall created by WTO is the wall of the trade related intellectual property rights agreement. (TRIPS). This too is part of a centrally planned authoritarian rule. As [agricultural company] Monsanto admitted, in drafting the agreement, the corporations organised as the Intellectual Property Committee were the "patients, diagnosticians and physicians all in one." Instead of telling the story of TRIPS and how corporate and WTO led globalisation is forcing India to dismantle its democratically designed patent laws, creating monopolies on seeds and medicines, pushing farmers to suicide and denying victims of AIDS, Cancer, TB, and Malaria access to life saving drugs, Friedman engages in another dishonest step to create a flat world.

He presents the open source Software Movement initiated by Richard Stallman, as a flattening trend of corporate globalisation when Stallman is a leading critic of intellectual property and corporate

> **FAST FACT**
>
> India's National Commission for Enterprises in the Unorganised Sector (NCEUS) reported in 2007 that 77 percent of people in India, approximately 836 million people, live on less than fifty cents a day.

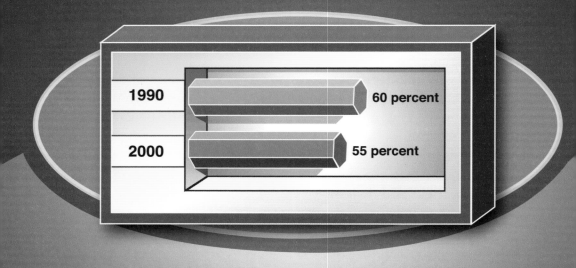

Farmers in India, as a Percentage of the Population

1990	60 percent
2000	55 percent

Taken from: 1990 and 2000 India Census, www.census.india.net. www.thesouthasian.org/archives/2005/where_are_50_million_farmers.html.

monopolies, and a fighter against the walls corporations are creating to prevent farmers from saving seeds, researchers from doing research, and software developers from creating new software. By presenting open sourcing in the same category as outsourcing and off shore production, Friedman hides corporate greed, corporate monopolies and corporate power, and presents corporate globalisation as human creativity and freedom.

A False Picture of Globalisation

This is deliberate dishonesty, not just [the] result of flat vision. That is why in his stories from India he does not talk [to] Dr. [Yusuf] Hamid of CIPLA [pharmaceutical company] who provided AIDS medicine to Africa for $200 when U.S. corporations wanted to sell them for $20,000 and who has called WTO's patent laws "genocidal". And in spite of Friedman's research team having fixed an appointment with me to fly down to Bangalore to talk about farmers' suicides for the documentary Friedman refers to, Friedman cancelled the appointment at the last minute.

Telling a one sided story for a one sided interest seems to be Friedman's fate. That is why he talks of 550 million Indian youth overtaking Americans in a flat world. When the entire information technology/outsourcing sector in India employs only a million out of a 1.2 billion people. Food and farming, textiles and clothing, health and education are nowhere in Friedman's monoculture of mind locked into IT [information technology].

Friedman presents a 0.1% picture and hides 99.9%. And in the 99.9% are Monsanto's seed monopolies and the suicides of thousands of wars. In the eclipsed 99.9% are the 25 million women who disappeared in high growth areas of India because a commodified world has rendered women a dispensable sex. In the hidden 99.9% economy are thousands of tribal children in Orissa, Maharashtra, Rajasthan who died of hunger because the public distribution system for food has been dismantled to create markets for agribusiness. The world of the 99.9% has grown poorer because of the economic globalisation.

EVALUATING THE AUTHORS' ARGUMENTS:

In this viewpoint Shiva disagrees with Thomas L. Friedman, interviewed in the next viewpoint, who claims the world is "flat." What do you think her response would be to his claim that in this new era of globalization the small have the opportunity to act big?

Globalization Has an Equalizing Effect

Thomas L. Friedman, interviewed by Nayan Chanda

"The small can act really big in the flat world."

In the following viewpoint Nayan Chanda interviews Thomas L. Friedman, who claims that globalization is having an equalizing effect around the globe—"flattening" the earth. Friedman argues that we have entered the third era of globalization, making the earth smaller than ever. In this era, he claims, companies are getting bigger and more efficient while, at the same time, access to getting into business is easier for everyone. Chanda is editor of *YaleGlobal Online* magazine at the Yale Center for the Study of Globalization. Friedman is a journalist for the *New York Times* and the author of *The World Is Flat*.

AS YOU READ, CONSIDER THE FOLLOWING QUESTIONS:

1. According to Friedman, during what years did the first era of globalization occur?
2. Which two large companies does Friedman identify as being sources of understanding globalization?
3. What example does Friedman use to explain his view that the small can act big in the new era of globalization?

ayan Chanda:
We have Tom [Thomas L.] Friedman with us this after-noon, to talk about his new book, The World Is Flat. *This book is third in a series he has been writing about globalization. Your first book, which was a kind of landmark, was* Lexus and the Olive Tree. *Since the publication of that book, how has the world changed? What is the most important change you've seen?*

Three Eras of Globalization

Tom Friedman:

Well you know the way I would locate this book, Nayan, is that I would argue that there have been three great eras of globalization. One I would call, for shorthand, Globalization 1.0. That was from about 1492 till 1800 when we saw the beginning of global arbitrage—Columbus discovers America, so basically that era shrunk the world from a size large to a size medium. The dynamic element in globalization in that era, was countries globalizing, for imperial reasons, for resources.

The second great era was 1800 till the year 2000—it just ended. And that era shrunk the world from a size medium to a size small. And that era was really spearheaded by companies globalizing, for markets and for labor. Now I would argue *Lexus and the Olive Tree* was really about the tail end of that era.

"Olive Tree" was nation-states, and "Lexus" was technology, and the book was about the interaction between what was new, this form of globalization that was shrinking the world from size medium to size small, and at the same time these traditional, ethnic, national issues. Now, what I discovered by visiting India in 2004 was that we'd actually entered a whole new era of globalization. And *Lexus* was wonderful for what it was, but it was out of date! It couldn't tell the whole story anymore, it couldn't explain the world, because what I really found in going to India was that we'd entered Globalization 3.0. And it's shrinking the world from size small to size tiny, and flattening the global economic playing field at the same time. And so this book builds on the shoulders of *Lexus*, in that sense, but it's really about the next stage.

Pulitzer Prize–winning journalist Thomas L. Friedman contends that because of globalization companies have become more efficient and that finding business opportunities is easier for everyone.

Inside the Companies of Globalization

Reading the book, one gets the impression that you took a dive into the innards of globalization and came out with some amazing tales of how things are happening behind the scenes that we don't see. Could [you] tell a little bit about what main things you saw, the main forces changing the globalized world today?

You know, you've got it exactly right, Nayan, in that [in] doing this book, I didn't really read a bunch of other books, I really dove into the companies themselves who were spearheading this process. And the book, in that sense, is very inductive. You know, I looked at what companies were doing and then tried to tease out the general patterns.

To begin with, my primary tutors for this book, were two Indian entrepreneurs: the president of Wipro, Vivec Paul, and the CEO of Infosys, Nandan Nilekani. So, how did I happen to end up with two Indian entrepreneurs? (And these are the heads really of the two cutting-edge, high-tech/outsourcing companies.) It's because they're actually at the epicenter of it now. And they could see the whole playing field. So to begin with, the book is different in that the people I tapped into were very different from *Lexus and the Olive Tree*, which was really a lot about Silicon Valley, and that perspective (not that I didn't also draw on that for this book).

Secondly, I really dove into some key companies that are now globalizing and are really the source for understanding globalization. Wal-Mart, UPS—these are companies we don't traditionally think of as being goldmines of insights into globalization, but in fact if you understand what's going on inside these companies, you can get an amazing view of the flattening of the global playing field and the forces that are doing it.

Both these companies you mention, they do not produce anything. They agglomerate or repackage others' products. So in this agglomeration or repackaging, how are they tapping the resources from this flat world. How does it happen?

Well, in the case of Wal-Mart, Wal-Mart's great innovation, as you say, is that Wal-Mart doesn't make anything. But what they do is draw products from all over the world and get them into stores at incredibly low prices. How do they do that? Through a global

supply chain that has been designed down to the last atom of efficiency. So as you take an item off the shelf in New Haven, Connecticut, another of that item will immediately be made in Xianjin, China. So there's perfect knowledge and transparency throughout that supply chain.

In the case of UPS, they've designed a global delivery system that allows them to deliver their products with that same efficiency; they are so efficient that they literally have a phenomena at UPS called "end-of-runway services." Think about that: "end of runway services." What do they do? Right before your product gets shipped, right at the end of the runway (almost literally—it's in the hangar, it's not literally at the end of the runway, but it could be at the end of the runway), they'll attach something; they'll attach a new lens to your camera, they'll add a special logo to your tennis shoes, they'll design it just for you, and they'll slap that on at the end of the runway. That's how efficient these systems have become. And of course, when you put them all together, you get a very flat global playing field.

Worries About Wal-Mart

Now of course, there have been a lot of criticisms of the business model of Wal-Mart, because it is driven by the single motive: maximizing profits for shareholders. And in the process, of course, they give products at a cheap price to the consumers. But people are complaining that this model leaves the workers out of the equation—workers not just in the United States, but perhaps also from China or anywhere else where they are procuring it from. So, is this a good model to promote?

Well, Wal-Mart to me, Nayan, really demonstrates one of the phenomenas of a flat world. I would call it "multiple-identity disorder." Now let me explain. I have to tell you, the consumer in me loves Wal-Mart. Wow, you can go there and get really quality goods at really low prices. And not just me, someone who's maybe an upper-income person. Some lower-income people are stretching their dollars further because of Wal-Mart. That's a big deal. The shareholder in me, Nayan, loves Wal-Mart. Let's assume I have it in my 401k somewhere. Wow, that stock's been a monster, so the shareholder in me loves Wal-Mart. The citizen in me, Nayan, hates Wal-Mart, because they only cover some 40 percent of their employees with health care, while Costco, their main competitor, charges a little bit more, but covers over 90 percent of their employees with health care. And when a Wal-Mart employee that doesn't have health care gets sick, what do they do? They go to the emergency ward at general hospital, and you know what happens then. Then we tax-payers pay their health care. And the neighbor in

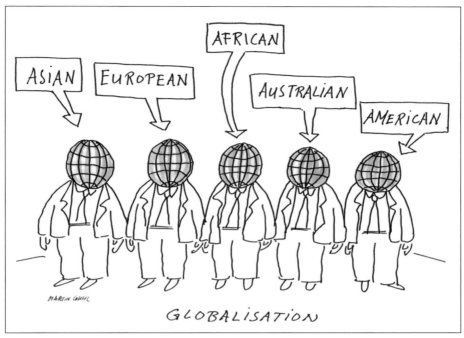

"'Globalization' Men with globes for heads labeled after the five continents," cartoon by Martin Guhl. Copyright © Martin Guhl. Reproduction rights obtainable from www.CartoonStock.com.

me, Nayan, is very disturbed about Wal-Mart. Disturbed about stories about how they've discriminated against women, disturbed about stories that they've locked employees into their stores overnight, disturbed about how they pay some of their employees. So when it comes to Wal-Mart, Nayan, I've got multiple identity disorder, because the shareholder and the consumer in me feels one thing, and the citizen and the neighbor in me feel something quite different. . . .

How do you resolve the dissonance you have between the citizen in you and the consumer in you?

I think we have to resolve that through social activism. I really support consumer activism that will say to Wal-Mart, that we as neighbors and consumers will say to Wal-Mart, "I love your low prices, but you know what? We're ready to spend five cents more, and we're ready to give you that five cents if you'll use two of those five cents to cover more of your employees with health care." That, to me, is where citizen activism really has to come into play.

Talking about citizen activism, one of the themes of your book is, because of this flattening of the world, it's harder to challenge from below, and the top-down structure is flattening into horizontal corporate positions. Now, these people who are being left behind, left out of this flattening process, how do they challenge the hierarchy? How do they join the flat world?

Well, those are two really different questions. Because if you ask, how do they challenge them, we see in our business (the news business) that thanks to the flat world, everyone can be a publisher, and an editor, and a journalist, all into one, through blogging. So you and I both could go out and start Nayan.com, or Tom.com, or TomandNayan.com, and suddenly we'd be in business. And if we're clever and witty and interesting, we'll get a global following. And then one day, once we've got our global following, if we see Dan Rather make a mistake on CBS News, we don't have to write a letter to the editor. No, TomandNayan.com will publish their own expose of Dan Rather. And if we've got our facts right, we can help bring Dan Rather down.

The thing you wanted to understand about the flattening of the world is, it enables the big to act really small. Think about Wal-Mart. With RFID [radio frequency identification] technology, they can tell you when Hispanics like to buy milk, as opposed to, you know, [when] other anglos prefer to buy milk as opposed to [when] African-Americans prefer to buy milk. Because they know their store is in predominantly Hispanic neighborhoods, black neighborhoods, or white neighborhoods. They know, they can actually trace, at a micro-level, they can act so small, Nayan, it's scary. The other side of it, though, is that the small can act really big in the flat world. TomandNayan.com, we can go out and be publishers, and if we get a following, man, we can act really big.

> **EVALUATING THE AUTHOR'S ARGUMENTS:**
>
> In this viewpoint Friedman says that the information for his book on globalization came primarily from two CEOs in India. Does this admission change the way you view his claims about globalization?

Globalization Requires Some Protectionism of National Economies

Clive Hamilton

> "*National governments have . . . ceded a large measure of their sovereignty over economic management to global financial markets.*"

In the following viewpoint Clive Hamilton argues that national governments have lost much of their sovereignty because of globalization, "the process by which the economies of the world have become increasingly interdependent through flows of capital and trade." According to Hamilton, "Domestic economic policy [of national governments] has been wholly reoriented over the last twenty years to satisfy the requirements of this global competition for capital." Economic measures instituted to appease global economic markets have resulted in more unemployment, stagnation of incomes, insecurity of jobs, longer working hours, and fewer services provided by the public sector. Foreign policy and relations have also "become increasingly dominated by the pursuit of narrow trade and investment interests." This leads national governments to countenance human rights abuses of their

Clive Hamilton, "A Great Unified World," *Arena Magazine,* vol. 34, April/May 1998, pp. 40(3). Copyright © 1998 Arena Printing and Publications Pty. Ltd.

trading partner countries, and this contributes to the moral decline of the country that countenances the abuse. Individual reluctance to accept abuses is countered by the concept of technological and cultural convergence, in which all nations develop common goals and ways of thinking as trade goes on, so that abuses decline as incomes rise. However, convergence is only partial, representing the adoption by the elite of the developing nations of certain materialistic Western values but not of Western views on human rights, which are rejected as "culturally inappropriate." However, if one were to ask the ordinary person in the trading partner country, one would find outrage at the abuses and a desire for the protection of their human rights. In conclusion, Hamilton hopes for a reevaluation "which leads us to take back some control of our national economies from international financial markets, transcend the fetishism of the economic, and reassert ethical values over economic values in our domestic and foreign policies." The following viewpoint was first delivered as an address to the Conference of the Medical Association for the Prevention of War at Australian National University, on April 26, 1997. Clive Hamilton is executive director of the Australia Institute and has a PhD in economics from the University of Sussex.

AS YOU READ, CONSIDER THE FOLLOWING QUESTIONS:
1. What is globalization, according to the author?
2. According to Hamilton, what does the idea of convergence provide?
3. What is a critical feature of diplomatic rationalism, according to the author?

Globalisation has transformed the world in ways truly unimaginable only twenty years ago. These changes are forcing us to reassess the foundations of democratic society, the welfare of the disadvantaged and the way we see the rest of the world.

Globalisation is the process by which the economies of the world have become increasingly interdependent through flows of capital and trade, and through transborder asset ownership. The flourishing of transnational corporations and the boom in world financial markets have been at the centre of this.

In the face of the fantastic growth of international financial flows and the speculative herd behaviour that goes with it, national governments of even the strongest countries now have greatly diminished influence over domestic economic policy, and small countries are largely powerless. In all countries, domestic economic policy has been wholly reoriented over the last twenty years to satisfy the requirements of this global competition for capital. Globalisation represents a sustained assault on national sovereignty and therefore on democracy itself. The citizen has become subject to the financier to a degree hitherto unknown.

The international auction has been mirrored by a domestic political auction, with conservative and social democratic parties competing to establish which can integrate the national economy into the world economy more quickly and effectively. Social democratic and labour parties have abandoned any alternative programme of social and economic change, and have single-mindedly pursued business investment and economic growth as the principal means of tackling poverty and unemployment, despite the manifest failure of that approach.

National governments have thus ceded a large measure of their sovereignty over economic management to global financial markets. Central banks are mostly weak, and are constrained to steer a narrow course through a canyon built by global capital markets. Governments frame budgets with the reactions of credit ratings agencies and foreign investors in mind. Global markets expect and enforce a range of economic and social policy measures believed to be in their interests. When unemployment increases, the markets generally rally because higher unemployment reduces the likelihood of inflation. If governments increase spending on social welfare they are in danger of being punished by capital withdrawals, especially if the new spending is to be financed by increased taxes on capital or wealth.

FAST FACT

According to the International Monetary Fund's *World Economic Outlook* in October 2008, the world economy was entering a major downturn in the face of the failure of the financial markets in rich countries.

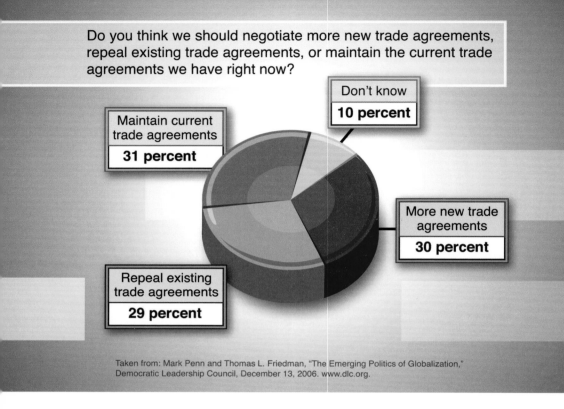

American Views on Trade

Do you think we should negotiate more new trade agreements, repeal existing trade agreements, or maintain the current trade agreements we have right now?

Don't know
10 percent

Maintain current trade agreements
31 percent

More new trade agreements
30 percent

Repeal existing trade agreements
29 percent

Taken from: Mark Penn and Thomas L. Friedman, "The Emerging Politics of Globalization," Democratic Leadership Council, December 13, 2006. www.dlc.org.

The political implications of globalisation and its ideological hand-maiden, economic rationalism, are profound. The panoply of economic measures to appease the markets (fiscal rectitude, trade liberalisation, microeconomic reform, privatisation and financial and labour market deregulation) has been applied vigorously in the 1980s and 1990s. Almost without exception, these policies have had an especially harsh impact on those with low incomes. Working people have watched as mass unemployment has become chronic and apparently incurable, real incomes have stagnated, jobs have become insecure, working hours have become longer and more intense, the extent and quality of services provided by the public sector have declined, neighbourhoods have become less safe, a generation of young people has been abandoned, and the safety net provided by many local communities has all but vanished.

Working people have been harangued by political leaders with a new and disturbing message. They must make sacrifices; they have been living beyond their means; financial incentives rather than social objectives are what really matter; they cannot rely on the state to support them; there is no choice but to integrate into the world economy; we must judge our economic policies by the reactions of foreign financiers; the sale of our assets to overseas interests is good for us (and besides is unavoidable); and it is a mistake to assume a secure and prosperous future for our children. At a time when working people more than ever need their governments to protect them from the worst ravages of international economic forces, this support has been withdrawn.

The dominance of economic rationalism over domestic policy formation has a counterpart in the formulation of foreign policy. I call it diplomatic rationalism.

In the belief that economics is all, our foreign relations have become increasingly dominated by the pursuit of narrow trade and investment interests. As a result, the Australian Government has shown that it is willing to turn its face away from human-rights abuses. Recently, we have seen a particularly craven instance of this in our dealings with China, where the merest hint of problems with access to Chinese markets has seen Australia refuse to support UN [United Nations] resolutions against human-rights abuses in that country. What concerns me at least as much as our refusal to support democratic forces in China and Indonesia is the impact on our own country of our failure to take a firm ethical position on these issues. I am concerned that diplomatic rationalism, as a critical part of the broader influence of economic rationalism, is eroding the moral strength and, quite possibly, the democratic institutions of Australia.

An intellectual justification of diplomatic rationalism is found in the idea of 'convergence'. Former foreign minister Gareth Evans endorsed convergence in the following terms in 1995:

> Underlying all the economic activity, and contributing mightily to it . . . has been the phenomenon of technological and cultural convergence, whereby countries of very different backgrounds are developing—under the particular impact of modern communications technology—information bases, practices,

institutions, tastes and outlooks that are ever more similar. We have come to do things more alike, see things more alike, and develop institutions and processes that are more alike in how we conduct business, administer governments, absorb information and enjoy our leisure.

The idea of convergence at once provides a grand theory of modern history, a mechanism that will take Australia into Asia, and a justification for the unashamed pursuit of economic self-interest. It provides a justification for diplomatic rationalism because it allows its adherents to believe that the abuses of human rights and denial of democratic forms that appear to be endemic to the way some societies function will ineluctably fade away as incomes rise. The political processes that will bring about these social and political transformations are not always clear, however.

The idea of some great unified world in which we all share common goals, ways of thinking, preferences, institutions, values and worldviews has a frightening Orwellian quality to it. It denies the value of diversity and it suggests a world more easily dominated by a few. It is ironic that the same politicians who appeal to convergence with Asia, at the same time strongly endorse multiculturalism within Australia. Why is diversity celebrated within a nation, but convergence welcomed between nations?

The idea of convergence is actually a product of the partial Westernisation of Asian middle classes (the pursuit of consumer-oriented life-styles, mimicking Western ways of presenting the self, adoption of Western symbols of success, absorption of popular Western culture, the replacement of more traditional family relationships with urbanised nuclear forms, a drift away from religious modes of social life and pursuit of self-interest. Often these Western characteristics are pursued in a more exaggerated and uncritical form than in the West itself.

It is not simply the case that Western nations are imposing these values on local cultures that do not want them. They have been welcomed by the new elites, or at least seen as inevitable. Convergence, then, is about a convergence of worldviews among elites, not a convergence of whole cultures. Simplifying somewhat, we can identify a dual process in which Asian elites adopt Western materialism and consumer life-styles, while rejecting 'Western' concepts of human rights as culturally inappropriate.

A critical feature of diplomatic rationalism is the way it homogenises societies and thinks always in terms of uniform national economic and other interests. While we recognise class, ethnic and political differences in our own country, we deal with other countries as though their governments represent homogeneous societies devoid of conflict. Of course, recognition of this conflict immediately raises the question of the legitimacy of governments and thus the legitimacy of our dealings with them, an uncomfortable question which diplomatic rationalists avoid. Any doubts about legitimacy can somehow be thrown out if it can be shown that the government in question is responsible for a high rate of economic growth. Australia's Indonesia policy is based on this fundamental confusion of the ruling regime with the society, of the government with the nation.

Several arguments are put in favour of suppressing, deferring or reinterpreting human rights. We are often told that human rights are specific to cultures and we should not try to impose Western values on other cultures. This view is vigorously promoted by ruling elites; it is designed to exploit nationalistic sentiment. Our own foreign affairs establishment tells us that it is unreasonable to impose Western perceptions of human rights on different cultural and political systems. The argument seems to underpin the Australian Government's attempts to defend its policy towards Indonesia.

In my own experience, if you talk to ordinary Indonesians (office workers, drivers, students, language teachers, porters, shop assistants) they are outraged at the abuses of human rights in their country, and would welcome the introduction of basic rights such as freedom from arbitrary arrest, protection against official violence and extortion, the rule of law, freedom of speech and the right to organise. At bottom, they have an essential yearning for some basic justice. This is a human trait, not a Western one, and to argue otherwise is essentially racist.

Globalisation has transformed not only the world economy but our politics and our moral judgement. The promised rewards (higher growth and living standards) have not materialised. Even if they had we must ask whether the price in human dignity would have been worth it.

I hope that we are entering an era of reevaluation, one which leads us to take back some control of our national economies from international financial markets, transcend the fetishism of the economic, and reassert ethical values over economic values in our domestic and foreign policies.

EVALUATING THE AUTHORS' ARGUMENTS:

In this viewpoint Hamilton argues that lower-income people have suffered, the "promised rewards [of globalization] (higher growth and living standards) have not materialized," and moral judgment has declined because of globalization. Compare Hamilton's argument with that of Daniel T. Griswold, in the following viewpoint, that any economic downturn in the United States is not the fault of globalization. Support the claims of one author against the other, using evidence from both.

Globalization Moderates Changes in National Economies

Daniel T. Griswold

"The era of globalization has brought healthy long-term growth and a moderation of the business cycle."

In the following viewpoint Daniel T. Griswold worries that globalization will be blamed for any recession in the U.S. economy. He argues that globalization is not the cause of economic slowdown and that, in fact, globalization has made the economy more stable and less likely to have a prolonged downturn. Griswold claims that the diversified markets of the globalized economy help nations weather economic slowdowns without major crises that they otherwise might not have avoided if they were completely dependent on a domestic economy only. Griswold is director of the Center for Trade Policy Studies at the Cato Institute.

AS YOU READ, CONSIDER THE FOLLOWING QUESTIONS:
1. Griswold claims that the United States has suffered how many recessions since the end of World War II?

Daniel T. Griswold, "Worried About a Recession? Don't Blame Free Trade," *Free Trade Bulletin,* March 31, 2008. Republished with permission of The Cato Institute, conveyed through Copyright Clearance Center, Inc.

2. According to a study cited by the author, a country needs to increase trade by how much to be one-third less likely to suffer sudden economic slowdowns or other crises?
3. The percent of profits that U.S. companies earn abroad have grown by how much since the 1960s, according to the author?

S peculation is growing that the U.S. economy may have already slipped into recession. If the past is any guide, politicians on the campaign trail will be tempted to blame trade and globalization for the passing pain of the business cycle. Rising unemployment and falling output can provide fertile ground for attacks on imports and foreign investment by U.S. multinational companies. But an analysis of previous recessions and expansions shows that international trade and investment are not to blame for downturns in the economy and may in fact be moderating the business cycle.

Economic Recessions

Economic downturns have occurred periodically throughout U.S. history. The popular definition of a recession is two consecutive quarters of negative growth in the nation's gross domestic product (GDP). The National Bureau of Economic Research [NBER] in Cambridge, Massachusetts, which has become the official bookkeeper of the business cycle, offers a more refined definition: "A recession is a significant decline in activity spread across the economy, lasting more than a few months, visible in industrial production, employment, real income, and wholesale-retail trade."

By NBER's accounting, the nation has suffered through 11 recessions since the end of World War II, not including the current possible downturn. All recessions produce, to one degree or another, falling industrial output, lower real wages and household income, higher rates of unemployment, increased foreclosures and bankruptcies, and growing self-doubt about our economy and our country's future. In the political arena, recessions often spur a backlash against incumbent office holders, especially those of the president's party, and against foreign producers and foreign trade in general.

The supposed link between trade and recessions is superficially appealing. During any recession, critics can point to imports that displace domestic production, putting some U.S. workers out of their jobs and supposedly reducing domestic demand for goods and services. They can more easily blame U.S. multinational corporations for "shipping our jobs overseas" by locating production facilities in countries where labor and other costs are lower. But like so much of the conventional wisdom about trade and the economy, the alleged link between rising levels of trade and recessions simply does not exist.

"The Great Moderation"

In recent decades, as foreign trade and investment have been rising as a share of the U.S. economy, recessions have actually become milder and less frequent. The softening of the business cycle has become so striking that economists now refer to it as "The Great Moderation." The more benign trend appears to date from the mid-1980s. . . .

Moderation of the business cycle has not come at the expense of overall growth. In the past 25 years (1983–2007), annual real GDP growth has averaged 3.3 percent. That is virtually the same average annual growth rate as occurred during the previous 25

Economic Contractions Are Becoming Less Common

Time Period	Number of Contractions	Average Length		Percentage of Time in Contraction
		Contractions	Expansions	
1855–1944	21	21 months	29 months	41
1945–1982	9	11 months	45 months	21
1983–2007	2	8 months	95 months	5

Taken from: Daniel T. Griswold, "Worried About a Recession? Don't Blame "Free Trade," *Free Trade Bulletin*, March 31, 2008.

years (1958–1982). Like a superior investment, our more globalized economy has delivered the same rate of return in the form of real GDP growth but with much less volatility than in the past. . . .

America's recent experience of a more globalized and less volatile economy has not been unique in the world. Other countries that have opened themselves to global markets have been less vulnerable to financial and economic shocks. Countries that put all their economic eggs in the domestic basket lack the diversification that a more globally integrated economy can fall back on to weather a slowdown. A study by Jeffrey Frankel and Eduardo Cavallo for NBER found that a country that increases trade as a share of its gross domestic product by 10 percentage points is actually about one-third less likely to suffer sudden economic slowdowns or other crises than if it were less open to trade. As the authors conclude:

> Some may find this counterintuitive: trade protectionism does not "shield" countries from the volatility of world markets as proponents might hope. On the contrary . . . economies that trade less with other countries are more prone to sudden stops and to currency crises.

FAST FACT

In March 2009 the World Bank warned that protectionism was on the rise across the globe since the financial crisis plunged the world into recession, despite government promises to avoid moves that restrict global trade.

A More Diversified and Flexible Economy

Globalization is not the only possible cause behind the moderation of the business cycle. Improved monetary policy, fewer external shocks (what some economists call "good luck"), and other structural changes in the economy may have all played a role. For example, the decline in unionization and the resulting increase in labor-market flexibility have allowed wages and employment patterns to adjust more readily to changing market conditions, mitigating spikes in unemployment. Better inventory management through just-in-time delivery has

The Cato Institute's Daniel T. Griswold (right) claims in the viewpoint that the diversification of global markets helps nations weather domestic economic slowdowns.

reduced the cyclical overhangs that can disrupt production. Lifting the ceiling on deposit interest rates has helped lending institutions weather downturns, while more access to consumer credit and home equity loans have helped families smooth their consumption patterns over time when incomes temporarily fall.

Combined with those other factors, expanding trade and globalization have helped to moderate swings in national output by blessing us with a more diversified and flexible economy. Exports can take up slack when domestic demand sags, and imports can satisfy demand when domestic productive capacity is reaching its short-term limits. Access to foreign capital markets can allow domestic producers and consumers alike to more easily borrow to tide themselves over during difficult times.

During the current economic turmoil, as the housing and mortgage markets have turned downward, many U.S. companies have maintained or expanded production by serving growing global markets. In 2007, U.S. exports of goods and services rose a brisk 12.6 percent from the year before, more than double the growth rate of imports. Meanwhile, U.S. companies and investors saw their earnings on foreign assets grow an even faster 20.3 percent.

A weakening dollar has helped to boost exports and earnings abroad, but the main driver of success overseas has been strong growth and lower trade barriers outside the United States. As *The Wall Street Journal* summarized in a front-page story: "Economies in most other parts of the world—including China, Latin America and Europe—have grown faster than the U.S. over the past 18 months, providing a countercyclical balance for multinational companies. Overseas growth could provide further support for companies and investors if parts of the U.S. economy continue to worsen."

American companies have been earning a larger and larger share of their profits overseas for decades now. According to economist Ed Yardeni, the share of profits that U.S. companies earn abroad has increased steadily from about 5 percent in the 1960s to about a quarter of all profits today.

Even the American icon Harley-Davidson motorcycle company in Milwaukee, Wisconsin, has become a multinational enterprise. The company that once came begging to Washington for protection from foreign competition is enjoying robust sales and profits abroad even as its domestic sales slump. In the second quarter of 2007, the company saw its profits jump by 19 percent—fueled by the double-digit growth in sales in Europe, Japan, and Canada—while its domestic sales fell 5.5 percent.

Earning a larger share of profits abroad allows Harley-Davidson and other U.S. companies to better weather downturns at home, reducing the need for drastic cost cutting and layoffs when recessions hit.

Do Not Blame Globalization

If the U.S. economy does tip into recession this year [2008], free trade and globalization will be among the likely scapegoats. The pain of recession will be real for millions of American households, but raising barriers to foreign trade and investment will provide no relief for most affected workers. In fact, reverting to protectionism would only reduce the capacity of our economy to regain its footing and resume its long-term pattern of growth.

For the U.S. economy as a whole, the era of globalization has brought healthy long-term growth and a moderation of the business cycle. Expansions are longer if less spectacular than in eras past, and downturns are mercifully shorter, shallower, and less frequent. Moderation of the business cycle in recent decades is something to be thankful for, and expanding trade and globalization deserve a share of the credit.

EVALUATING THE AUTHOR'S ARGUMENTS:

Griswold cites data in support of his view that globalization should not be blamed for any economic recession. What kind of new information or different data would argue in favor of the view that globalization was, in fact, to blame for an economic downturn?

Facts About Globalization

Editor's note: These facts can be used in reports or papers to reinforce or add credibility when making important points or claims.

Activities of Economic Globalization
- International trade: importing and exporting of goods between nations.
- Foreign direct investment: companies from one country building factories in other countries.
- International capital flows: investment across national borders.

The A.T. Kearney/*Foreign Policy* Globalization Index Top 10 Globalized Countries
Based on Economic Integration, Personal Contact, Technological Connectivity, and Political Engagement, 2007

1. Singapore
2. Hong Kong
3. Netherlands
4. Switzerland
5. Ireland
6. Denmark
7. United States
8. Canada
9. Jordan
10. Estonia

World Trade Organization Global Trade Statistics
Growth in Volume of Trade, 2000–2007 (Annual Percentage Change)

- North America: exports 3 percent; imports 4 percent
- South and Central America: exports 6.5 percent; imports 8 percent
- Europe: exports 4 percent; imports 3.5 percent

- Commonwealth of Independent States: exports 8 percent; imports 17 percent
- Asia: exports 10.5 percent; imports 8.5 percent

Leading Exporters, 2007

1. Germany
2. China
3. United States
4. Japan
5. France

Leading Importers, 2007

1. United States
2. Germany
3. China
4. Japan
5. United Kingdom

World Bank Global Wealth Statistics
Percentage of World Gross Domestic Product by Region, 2005

- High-income countries: 60 percent
- East Asia and Pacific: 13 percent
- Latin America and Caribbean: 8 percent
- Europe and Central Asia: 7 percent
- South Asia: 5 percent
- Middle East and North Africa: 3 percent
- Sub-Saharan Africa: 2 percent

Change in Percentage of World Output, 1995 to 2006

- High-income countries: 66 percent to 59 percent
- East Asia and Pacific: 9 percent to 14 percent
- Latin America and Caribbean: 9 percent to 8 percent
- Europe and Central Asia: 7 percent to 8 percent
- South Asia: 4 percent to 6 percent
- Middle East and North Africa: 3 percent in both years
- Sub-Saharan Africa: 2 percent in both years

Organizations to Contact

The editors have compiled the following list of organizations concerned with the issues debated in this book. The descriptions are derived from materials provided by the organizations. All have publications or information available for interested readers. The list was compiled on the date of publication of the present volume; the information provided here may change. Be aware that many organizations take several weeks or longer to respond to queries, so allow as much time as possible.

Cato Institute
1000 Massachusetts Ave. NW
Washington, DC 20001-5403
(202) 842-0200
Web site: www.cato.org

The Cato Institute is a public policy research foundation dedicated to limiting the role of government, protecting individual liberties, and promoting free markets. The Center for Trade Policy Studies at the Cato Institute works to increase public understanding of the benefits of free trade and the costs of protectionism. Among the center's publications are the *Free Trade Bulletin* and numerous policy analyses and briefing papers on the topic of trade.

Center for Economic Policy Research (CEPR)
53–56 Great Sutton St.
London EC1V 0DG, United Kingdom
+44 (0)20 7183 8801
e-mail: cepr@cepr.org
Web site: www.cepr.org

CEPR is the leading European research network in economics. The center conducts research through a network of academic researchers and disseminates the results to the private sector and policy community.

CEPR produces a wide range of reports, books, and conference volumes each year, including "The Happy Few: The Internationalisation of European Firms."

Economic Policy Institute (EPI)
1333 H St. NW, Ste. 300, East Tower
Washington, DC 20005-4707
(202) 775-8810
e-mail: epi@epi.org
Web site: www.epi.org

EPI is a nonprofit Washington, D.C., think tank that seeks to broaden the discussion about economic policy to include the interests of low- and middle-income workers. EPI briefs policy makers at all levels of government; provides technical support to national, state, and local activists and community organizations; testifies before national, state, and local legislatures; and provides information and background to the print and electronic media. EPI publishes books, studies, issue briefs, popular education materials, and other publications, among which is the biennially published *State of Working America.*

Global Policy Forum (GPF)
777 UN Plaza, Ste. 3D
New York, NY 10017
(212) 557-3161
e-mail: gpf@globalpolicy.org
Web site: www.globalpolicy.org

GPF is a nonprofit organization with consultative status at the United Nations (UN). The mission of GPF is to monitor policy making at the UN, promote accountability of global decisions, educate and mobilize for global citizen participation, and advocate on vital issues of international peace and justice. GPF publishes policy papers, articles, and statements, including "Whose Partnership for Whose Development? Corporate Accountability in the UN System Beyond the Global Compact."

Human Rights Watch (HRW)
350 Fifth Ave., 34th Fl.
New York, NY 10118-3299
(212) 290-4700

e-mail: hrwnyc@hrw.org
Web site: www.hrw.org

HRW is dedicated to protecting the human rights of people around the world. The organization investigates human rights abuses, educates the public, and works to change policy and practice. Among its numerous publications is the report *The 2007 US Trade Policy Template: Opportunities and Risks for Workers' Rights.*

International Forum on Globalization (IFG)

1009 General Kennedy Ave., Ste. 2
San Francisco, CA 94129
(415) 561-7650
e-mail: ifg@ifg.org
Web site: www.ifg.org

IFG promotes equitable, democratic, and ecologically sustainable economies in the era of globalization. IFG produces numerous publications; organizes high-profile, large public events; hosts many issue-specific seminars; coordinates press conferences and media interviews at international events; and participates in many other activities that focus on the myriad consequences of globalization. Among its publications is *The Rise and Predictable Fall of Globalized Industrial Agriculture.*

International Trade Union Confederation (ITUC)

5 Boulevard du Roi Albert II, Bte 1
1210 Brussels, Belgium
+32 (0)2 224 0211
e-mail: info@ituc-csi.org
Web site: www.ituc-csi.org

ITUC is an international advocacy group for trade unions, supporting their mission to improve working conditions. The ITUC promotes and defends workers' rights and interests through international cooperation between trade unions, global campaigning, and advocacy within the major global institutions. Available at the ITUC's Web site are various publications and reports, including "The Role of the IFIs in Supporting Decent Work and Countering the Risks of Financial Globalisation."

Just Foreign Policy

4410 Massachusetts Ave. NW, Ste. 290
Washington, DC 20016

(202) 448-2898
e-mail: info@justforeignpolicy.org
Web site: www.justforeignpolicy.org

Just Foreign Policy is an independent and nonpartisan membership organization. Just Foreign Policy is dedicated to reforming U.S. foreign policy to serve the interests and reflect the values of the broad majority of Americans. The organization has legislative alerts and updates, as well as suggestions for political action, at its Web site.

Oxfam International
226 Causeway St., 5th Fl.
Boston, MA 02114-2206
(800) 77-OXFAM (776-9326)
e-mail: info@oxfamamerica.org
Web site: www.oxfam.org

Oxfam International is a confederation of organizations working to end poverty and injustice. Oxfam's trade campaign presses decision makers and governments for new trade rules that make a real and positive difference in the fight against poverty. Oxfam publishes numerous reports and press releases, available at its Web site.

Peter G. Peterson Institute for International Economics
1750 Massachusetts Ave. NW
Washington, DC 20036-1903
(202) 328-9000
e-mail: comments@petersoninstitute.org
Web site: www.iie.com

The Peter G. Peterson Institute for International Economics is a private, nonprofit, nonpartisan research institution devoted to the study of international economic policy. The institute seeks to provide timely and objective analysis of, and concrete solutions to, a wide range of international economic problems. The institute publishes numerous policy briefs available at its Web site, including *Islam, Globalization, and Economic Performance in the Middle East.*

Society for International Development (SID)
Via Panisperna 207
Rome, 00184 Italy

+39 0(6) 487 2172
Web site: www.sidint.org

SID is a global network of individuals and institutions concerned with development that is participative, pluralistic, and sustainable. The society works with more than one hundred associations, networks, and institutions involving academia, parliamentarians, students, political leaders, and development experts, both at local and international levels, to strive for a better world. SID gathers and disseminates information on innovative development published in papers and reports, including *Reflections on Development and Democracy in Africa.*

World Trade Organization (WTO)

Centre William Rappard, Rue de Lausanne 154, CH-1211
Geneva 21, Switzerland
+41 22 739 51 11
e-mail: enquiries@wto.org
Web site: www.wto.org

The WTO is the only global international organization dealing with the rules of trade between nations, with the goal of helping producers of goods and services, exporters, and importers conduct their business. The WTO sponsors trade agreements between member nations and supports trade liberalization. Among the information available at its Web site are the regional trade agreements, such as the North American Free Trade Agreement (NAFTA).

Worldwatch Institute

1776 Massachusetts Ave. NW
Washington, DC 20036
(202) 452-1999
e-mail: worldwatch@worldwatch.org
Web site: www.worldwatch.org

The Worldwatch Institute's mission is to generate and promote insights and ideas that empower decision makers to build an ecologically sustainable society that meets human needs. The institute seeks innovative solutions to intractable problems, emphasizing a blend of government leadership, private sector enterprise, and citizen action that can make a sustainable future a reality. The institute publishes *World Watch* magazine and numerous reports, including *Powering China's Development.*

For Further Reading

Books

Bhagwati, Jagdish N. *In Defense of Globalization.* New York: Oxford University Press, 2007. An internationally renowned economist takes on the critics of globalization, claiming that globalization is in fact the most powerful force for social good in the world today.

Cohen, Daniel. *Globalization and Its Enemies.* Cambridge, MA: MIT Press, 2007. Presents the problem of globalization as one of developing countries being excluded from the material prosperity they want, rather than a problem of exploitation.

Ellwood, Wayne. *The No-Nonsense Guide to Globalization.* Oxford, UK: New Internationalist, 2006. Examines the ways in which globalization can be both a force for equality, through access to information, and the embodiment of inequality, through the rich world's consumption of resources at the expense of poor countries.

Engler, Mark. *How to Rule the World: The Coming Battle over the Global Economy.* New York: Nation, 2008. Describes the conflict between a Bill Clinton–era vision of an expanding, corporate-controlled global economy and a George W. Bush–era imperial globalization based on U.S. military dominance.

Friedman, Thomas L. *The World Is Flat 3.0: A Brief History of the Twenty-First Century.* New York: Picador, 2007. Explores globalization's opportunities for individual empowerment, achievements at lifting millions out of poverty, and environmental, social, and political drawbacks.

Greenwald, Bruce C.N., and Judd Kahn. *Globalization: n. The Irrational Fear That Someone in China Will Take Your Job.* Indianapolis: Wiley, 2008. Cuts through some alleged myths surrounding globalization and looks more closely at what the authors take to be its real impact and its future consequences.

Hebron, Lui F., and John F. Stack Jr. *Globalization: Debunking the Myths.* Upper Saddle River, NJ: Prentice Hall, 2008. Presents arguments for and against globalization, examining a wide range of views on the economic, political, cultural, and environmental dimensions of globalization and their underlying frameworks, methodologies, and expectations.

Held, David, and Anthony McGrew. *Globalization/Anti-Globalization: Beyond the Great Divide*. Indianapolis: Polity, 2007. Tests the claims of those who dismiss the continuing significance of globalization through a comprehensive assessment of contemporary global trends, presenting the case for continuing to take globalization seriously.

Lechner, Frank J., and John Boli, eds. *The Globalization Reader*. Indianapolis: Wiley-Blackwell, 2007. A comprehensive introduction to globalization that attempts to convey its complexity, importance, and contentiousness from diverse vantage points.

Milanovic, Branko. *Worlds Apart: Measuring International and Global Inequality*. Princeton, NJ: Princeton University Press, 2007. Addresses just how to measure global inequality among individuals and shows that inequality is shaped by complex forces often working in different directions.

Rodrick, Dani. *One Economics, Many Recipes: Globalization, Institutions, and Economic Growth*. Princeton, NJ: Princeton University Press, 2008. Argues that neither globalizers nor antiglobalizers have got it right and shows how successful countries craft their own unique strategies.

Sachs, Jeffrey D. *The End of Poverty: Economic Possibilities for Our Time*. New York: Penguin, 2006. Offers a big-picture vision of the keys to economic success in the world today and the steps that are necessary to achieve prosperity for all.

Scholte, Jan Aart. *Globalization: A Critical Introduction*. New York: Palgrave Macmillan, 2005. Explores many dimensions of globalization with a core focus on the rise of supraterritoriality, or transborder relations, which the author argues is globalization's most distinctive feature.

Steger, Manfred. *Globalization: A Very Short Introduction*. New York: Oxford University Press, 2009. Goes beyond a narrow economic focus to cover all the major causes and consequences of globalization, as well as the hotly contested question of whether globalization is, ultimately, a good or a bad thing.

Stiglitz, Joseph E. *Making Globalization Work*. New York: W.W. Norton, 2007. Offers inventive solutions to a host of global problems, including the indebtedness of developing countries, international fiscal instability, and worldwide pollution.

Wolf, Martin. *Why Globalization Works*. New Haven, CT: Yale University Press, 2005. Explains how globalization works as a concept and how it operates in reality.

Periodicals

Aeppel, Timothy. "Overseas Profits Provide Shelter for U.S. Firms," *Wall Street Journal*, August 9, 2007.

Andrews, John. "A Duty to Defy Globalism," *Denver Post*, June 22, 2008.

Bailey, Ronald. "The Poor May Not Be Getting Richer: But They Are Living Longer, Eating Better, and Learning to Read," *Reason Online*, March 9, 2005. www.reason.com.

Bernstein, Jared, and Josh Bivens. "The Pain of Globalisation," *Guardian* (Manchester, UK), November 9, 2007.

Bhagwati, Jagdish N., and Arvind Panagariya. "Why the Trade Talks Collapsed," *Wall Street Journal*, July 7, 2007.

Blinder, Alan S. "Offshoring: The Next Industrial Revolution?" *Foreign Affairs*, March/April 2006.

Brooks, David. "The Cognitive Age," *New York Times*, May 2, 2008.

———. "Good News About Poverty," *New York Times*, November 27, 2004.

Bybee, Roger. "Globalization vs. Democracy: Huge Majority Seek Global Labor Standards," *Z*, November 2008. www.zmag.org.

Chua, Amy. "Globalizing Hate," *Amnesty International Magazine*, Summer 2003.

Decatur (AL) Daily. "Globalization Is Problematic; So Are Alternatives," July 3, 2008.

Dorn, James A. "Is Prosperity the Objective? Trade Is Far Better than Aid," *Investor's Business Daily*, January 14, 2004.

Engler, Mark. "The World Is Not Flat," *Dollars & Sense*, May/June 2008.

Francis, David R. "In Age of Outsourcing, Do the Old Rules Apply?" *Christian Science Monitor*, March 5, 2004.

Friedman, Thomas L. "Big Ideas and No Boundaries," *New York Times*, October 6, 2006.

———. "30 Little Turtles," *New York Times*, February 29, 2004.

———. "What Goes Around . . . ," *New York Times*, February 26, 2004.

Greider, William. "America's Truth Deficit," *New York Times*, July 18, 2005.

Griswold, Daniel T. "The U.S. Trade Deficit and Jobs: The Real Story," *Free Trade Bulletin*, no. 3, Cato Institute Center for Trade Policy Studies, February 3, 2003. www.freetrade.org.

Heymann, Jody, interviewed by Juliana Bunim. "Forgotten Families," *Mother Jones*, April 21, 2006. www.motherjones.com.

Hinkle, A. Barton. "Give and Take: Much-Maligned Globalization, Offshoring Give Jobs to Virginians," *Richmond Times-Dispatch*, May 22, 2007.

Investor's Business Daily. "The Backlash Against Globalization," July 24, 2007.

Kissinger, Henry A. "Falling Behind: Globalization and Its Discontents," *International Herald Tribune*, June 3, 2008.

Lendman, Stephen. "The War on Working Americans—Part II," OpEdNews.com, August 29, 2007. www.opednews.com.

Levinson, Marc. "Freight Pain: The Rise and Fall of Globalization," *Foreign Affairs*, November/December 2008.

Maira, Arun. "Globalisation and the Peepul Tree," *Economic Times*, June 9, 2005.

Marshall, Will. "Curing Globaphobia," *Blueprint*, January 4, 2007.

Michaels, Patrick J. "Will the U.N. Chill Out on Climate Change?" *National Review Online*, December 9, 2008. www.nationalreview.com.

Milanovic, Branko. "Developing Countries Worse Off than Once Thought—Part I," *YaleGlobal Online*, February 11, 2008. www.yaleglobal.yale.edu.

Record (Bergen County, NJ). "'Til You Drop: Consumerism and the Global Village," November 23, 2007.

Samuelson, Robert J. "Globalization Is a Reality—Deal with It," *Investor's Business Daily*, October 24, 2007.

Saul, John Ralston. "The Collapse of Globalism," *Harper's*, March 2004.

Steigerwald, Bill. "India Rising," *Pittsburgh Tribune-Review*, April 7, 2007.

Stiglitz, Joseph E. "A Progressive Response to Globalization," *Nation*, April 17, 2006.

Index

global trends in, *65*

Picture Credits

Maury Aaseng, 13, 21, 26, 34, 39, 55, 61, 65, 78, 84, 90, 100, 112, 119
AP Images, 10, 28, 53, 66, 82, 92, 96, 104, 112,
© Joe Baraban/Alamy, 41
Adam Berry/Bloomberg News/Landov, 76
Tomas Bravo/Reuters/Landov, 71
Alejandro Bringas/Reuters/Landov, 15
Kevin Dietsch/Landov, 121
Scott Gries/Getty Images for Chanel, 59
© Peter Horree/Alamy, 46
© ImageState/Alamy, 32
© The Print Collector/Alamy, 8
Kfir Sivan/Israel Sun/Landov, 50
© Jim West/Alamy, 87
Zhu Xiang/Xinhua/Landov, 22